# International Migrants and Refugees in Cape Town's Informal Economy

## SAMP MIGRATION POLICY SERIES No. 70

**Godfrey Tawodzera, Abel Chikanda, Jonathan Crush and Robertson Tengeh**

**Series Editor: Prof. Jonathan Crush**

Southern African Migration Programme (SAMP)
2015

AUTHORS

**Godfrey Tawodzera** is Senior Lecturer, Department of Geography, University of Limpopo

**Abel Chikanda** is Assistant Professor, Department of Geography, University of Kansas, Lawrence, USA

**Jonathan Crush** is CIGI Chair in Global Migration and Development, Balsillie School of International Affairs, Waterloo, Canada

**Robertson Tengeh** is Senior Lecturer, Cape Peninsula University of Technology, Cape Town

ACKNOWLEDGEMENTS

SAMP and its partners in the Growing Informal Cities Project would like to thank the IDRC for funding the project and this publication. The survey methodology was designed by a group of researchers that included Wade Pendleton (UCT), Caroline Skinner (UCT), Sally Peberdy (GCRO), Ines Raimundo (EMU), Ramos Muanamoha (EMU), Potsiso Phasha (GCRO), Paul Okwi (IDRC) and the authors of this report. Key informant interviews were conducted by Vanya Gastrow. Thanks are also due to Edgar Pieterse, Bronwen Dachs, Maria Salamone, Jane Battersby and Gareth Haysom.

Published by the Southern African Migration Programme, International Migration Research Centre, Balsillie School of International Affairs, Waterloo, Ontario, Canada

First published 2015

ISBN 978-1-920596-15-6

Cover photo by Thom Pierce for the Growing Informal Cities Project

Production by Bronwen Dachs Muller, Cape Town

Printed by Megadigital, Cape Town

CONTENTS          PAGE

## LIST OF TABLES

## LIST OF FIGURES

# EXECUTIVE SUMMARY

Attacks on migrant and refugee entrepreneurs and their properties by South African rivals and ordinary citizens have become a common phenomenon throughout the country, including the city of Cape Town. Business robberies often result in deaths or serious injuries. The Somali Community Board has noted that over 400 Somali refugees, many of them informal traders, were murdered in South Africa between early 2002 and mid-2010. The police are frequently accused by migrants of fomenting or turning a blind eye to xenophobic attacks on their businesses. Meanwhile, the government refuses to acknowledge the existence of xenophobia or the xenophobic rhetoric in many of these attacks, claiming instead that they are simply the actions of criminal elements. Photographs published in the media of the looting of migrant stores do not tend to feature hardened criminals, but ordinary citizens including children in school uniform.

Migrant businesses are portrayed by officials, citizens and the media as having a negative impact on the South African economy and undermining the livelihoods of South Africans. The prevalence of such perceptions helps to explain growing xenophobic sentiment against migrants and refugees. Contrary to these popular perceptions, an emerging literature on migrant entrepreneurship is beginning to demonstrate the positive economic contributions of migrants and refugees to the country. This report examines the nature of informal migrant and refugee entrepreneurship in Cape Town and whether or not the negative stereotypes have any validity. It also seeks to examine what economic contributions migrants and refugees make to the local economy.

The report is based on the research conducted by the Growing Informal Cities project, a partnership between SAMP/IMRC, the African Centre for Cities at the University of Cape Town, the Gauteng City-Region Observatory (GCRO) and Eduardo Mondlane University in Maputo. A questionnaire was administered to a sample of 518 migrant owners of micro-enterprises, which had to meet three basic criteria for inclusion: (a) owned by a non-South African; (b) in operation for at least two years; and (c) unregistered with the South African Revenue Services (SARS). Although migrant entrepreneurs are located in most areas of the city, certain areas have particular concentrations of migrant-owned businesses. The questionnaires were administered in four such areas: Imizamo Yethu, Philippi, Bellville, and Cape Town CBD. Thirty in-depth interviews were also conducted with selected owners of informal micro-enterprises. Two focus group discussions were held in the Cape Town

CBD and Philippi respectively. Fifteen key informant interviews were held with various stakeholders in Cape Town to understand the operation and constraints faced by migrants operating in the city's informal economy.

The major findings about the personal profile of the migrant and refugee entrepreneurs were as follows:

- The entrepreneurs came from over 20 different countries of which Zimbabwe, Somalia, the Democratic Republic of the Congo (DRC), Nigeria, Malawi, Ethiopia and Cameroon were the most prominent. Just over a third were from other countries in the SADC. The prominence of Zimbabwean entrepreneurs in the Cape Town informal economy is not surprising, given the events in that country over the past decade and a half and resultant mass migration to South Africa. A total of 57% of the entrepreneurs were from other African countries, especially the DRC, Somalia, Nigeria and Ethiopia. The majority of migrants from these countries (except Nigeria) came to South Africa as refugees.

- A third of the entrepreneurs had refugee permits. Of these, nearly 60% came from only three countries: the DRC, Ethiopia and Somalia. A further 31% held asylum-seeker permits. Of these, 32% were Zimbabwean while another 30% came from the DRC, Ethiopia and Somalia. Nearly 12% had permanent residence permits while 8% were holders of work permits. Only 7% of the respondents indicated that they did not have official documentation to stay in South Africa. Thus, the majority of migrant entrepreneurs are forced migrants who are entitled to human rights protection under international and South African refugee law.

- Very few of the entrepreneurs entered South Africa before 1994. Only 8% had arrived in the immediate post-apartheid years. While another 20% came in the period 2000 to 2004, the vast majority (70%) came during the last decade. As many as 44% arrived between 2005 and 2009 and a further 27% thereafter. Migration from Zimbabwe, in particular, escalated between 2005 and 2009 as the country plunged deeper into crisis.

- Despite the perception that unemployment at home is a driver of migration to South Africa, only 14% of the entrepreneurs were unemployed immediately before leaving for South Africa. Another 19% were students. Twenty-six percent were working in the informal economy in their home countries.

- Around 60% had worked in the formal sector since coming to South Africa primarily as unskilled manual workers (20%), skilled manual workers (11%), domestic workers

(10%), farmworkers (6%) and security workers (5%). Only 12% had experienced periods of unemployment and 7% had been students. Some had started informal businesses while they were still studying to help finance their studies while others started their business after finishing their education and failing to find formal employment.

There is a perception in South Africa, including in government, that migrant entrepreneurs have an innate ability or set of skills that makes them more skilled and competitive than South Africans. Understanding why people establish businesses is useful in understanding such entrepreneurial motivation. The survey sought to investigate how migrant entrepreneurs in Cape Town acquired the skills that they used in their business. The majority (64%) said that they were self-taught while 44% said they had learned skills from friends and relatives. Around a quarter (26%) had acquired skills from previous work experience. Less than 10% had formal skills training that they used in their business activity.

The survey concentrated on micro-enterprises in three major sectors: (a) retail, trade and wholesale; (b) manufacturing; and (c) services. About 62% of the entrepreneurs were engaged in retail, trade and wholesale activities, 28% in services and 10% in manufacturing. A number of migrant entrepreneurs were engaged in more than one sector; for example, manufacturing crafts as well as selling shoes. Their business strategies and activities included the following:

- Only a few of the businesses (less than 5%) were established before 2000. The majority (over 50%) started in 2010 and after. In general, the data suggests that in Cape Town the rapid growth of non-South Africans in the city's informal economy is a relatively recent phenomenon.

- Comparing the year in which the migrant came to South Africa with the year they established their business shows that there is a clear time lag between the two. Most migrants therefore do not establish a business as soon as they arrive.

- The most significant business location was a temporary stall on the street (38% of the total sample). Next was a permanent stall on the street (21%). Other fixed premises included workshops or shops (16%), their own home (11%), a permanent stall in a market (11%) and a shop in a house, yard or garage (3%). Other temporary sites of significance included taxi ranks (11%) and in the customer's home (3%). A total of 9% were mobile, predominantly selling goods door to door.

- Over 70% started their business on their own, without the assistance of others. Only 15% started the business with other migrants from their home countries, and 12% with members of their family. Only 4% reported starting with South African partners. Even fewer took over businesses that had been started by South Africans.

- The vast majority used their own savings to start the business. Most self-financing migrants used savings from prior employment. Other sources of start-up funds were loans from relatives (29%) and non-relatives, usually other migrants from their home country (16%). The use of both formal and informal financial institutions was limited, which emphasizes self-reliance and personal networks as sources of business start-up capital. Those who tried to get bank loans were invariably turned down.

- Once a business is established, very few of the entrepreneurs seek loans from other sources. The majority (83%) had not acquired a single loan in the previous 12 months. The growth of a business is almost entirely dependent on the reinvestment of profits from that business.

- The question is whether businesses are able to grow despite the absence of credit. The survey found that while more than two-thirds of the sample had less than ZAR10,000 to start their business, only 23% valued their current business at less than ZAR10,000. While only 7% had at least ZAR30,000 at start-up, nearly 30% valued their current business at more than ZAR30,000. This is evidence that most informal migrant entrepreneurs are able to scale up their business operations.

Migrants have long been portrayed by officials, citizens and the media as having a negative impact on the South African economy and undermining the livelihoods of South Africans. Contrary to these popular perceptions, this report demonstrates their positive economic contributions to Cape Town:

- Over a third of the informal entrepreneurs pay rent to the city council or municipality. Furthermore, 31% pay rent to the South African private owner of their business premises. Only a quarter of the respondents said they did not pay any rent. The average rent paid per month varied widely with a mean monthly rental of ZAR2,223. In total, the 362 respondents who paid rent collectively paid a mean monthly rent of ZAR805,000 or ZAR9.7 million per year.

- A large number of respondents indicated that they sourced their goods locally from wholesalers (63%), small shops and retailers (20%), supermarkets (15%) and from factories. A smaller number (11%) sourced produce (mainly fruit and vegetables) from the fresh produce market in Epping. Only a small proportion sourced the goods from another country (10%) or their home country (7%). This clearly indicates that migrant entrepreneurs play an important role in supporting South African businesses.

- Migrant entrepreneurs create jobs in Cape Town in three main ways. First, they buy goods from retailers and wholesalers and thus directly support the employees of South African-based manufacturers who sell their goods through local retailers and wholesalers. Second, they support local jobs at the wholesalers and retailers where they buy their goods. Third, they play an important role in direct hiring of people to work for them in their businesses.

- These entrepreneurs created a total of 644 jobs including family employment or 496 jobs for non-family. Of the non-family jobs, 282 (57%) went to South Africans. Of these, 41% were full-time jobs. As many as 41% of the entrepreneurs employed South Africans. There is a general preference for female South Africans in hiring. Not only are migrant entrepreneurs creating jobs for South Africans, they show a distinct and welcome gender bias in that they employ more female than male South Africans. In a labour market that discriminates against women, this contribution to greater gender equity should not be overlooked.

The report also examines the problems and challenges migrant entrepreneurs face in running a successful business operation in Cape Town. The main challenges faced by the migrant entrepreneurs, like business owners everywhere, are economic. Competition is fierce in the informal economy and half of the respondents said they had too many competitors. As many as 45% were affected by competition from supermarkets.

Migrant entrepreneurs also face significant security challenges. South Africa has an extremely high crime rate but there is evidence that migrants are disproportionately affected by violence. Some of this can be attributed to business competition. However, theft and looting of migrants businesses by ordinary citizens is also common. As many as 73% of the entrepreneurs saw crime and theft as a significant challenge to their operations. Physical attacks and assault by South Africans were of concern to 36% of the respondents. Some felt that they are systematically targeted because the criminals know that the police will not help. Many claimed that, even when crimes are reported, the police do not take action. A third cited confiscation of goods by the police as a problem and 15% cited physical assaults by the police.

Nearly 50% of the entrepreneurs mentioned discrimination against people of their nationality as a problem and a third that they had to endure verbal assaults from South

Africans. Forty-five percent said their business operations had been affected by xenophobia. Where a migrant comes from appears to influence how susceptible their business operations are to xenophobia. For example, 68% of Cameroonians, 66% of Somalis, 50% of Congolese, 49% of Ethiopians, 45% of Kenyans and 41% of Nigerians said their business was affected by xenophobia. By contrast, only 30% of Zimbabweans said their business was affected by xenophobia.

Cape Town Mayor, Patricia de Lille, has made several public pronouncements about the value of informal entrepreneurs to Cape Town's economy. It is not clear whether she includes migrant and refugee entrepreneurs in her statements. The Operation Fiela attack by the police and army on vendors at the Cape Town railway station in early 2015 certainly leaves room for doubt. However, she is also on record as stating that Cape Town's strategies, policies and by-laws on the informal economy should include everyone. This report goes beyond the rhetoric of inclusion to demonstrate with hard evidence exactly why migrant and refugee entrepreneurs should not be excluded but accepted as an integral and valuable part of the local economy.

# INTRODUCTION

Opening the 2013 City of Cape Town Summit on Informal Traders, Executive Mayor Patricia de Lille observed that "our strategy, which has as its goal economic growth for Cape Town, understands the layers of the market. It understands that there is a formal sector and an informal one and, while we may need to cater to each one differently, both of them must be central features of our policy decisions."[1] She continued in similarly positive vein that "it is often the energy generated by the informal sector that provides much of the cash flow, exchange and commodity consumption within large sectors of the respective populations. The critical element at the core is that the solvency of many communities, of many families, and of many individuals, is enabled by informal economic activity." Pledging the City's support for the informal economy, she concluded: "We need traders to be a part of the city and give their input on our policies, on our strategies, and on our by-laws so that they include everyone and do not exclude anyone."

The traders who ply the markets, streets and communities of Cape Town may see the Mayor's words of welcome for everyone in the informal economy as political rhetoric. Following nationwide xenophobic attacks on migrants and refugees in early 2015, the South African government launched "Operation Fiela", a thinly disguised attempt to make life even more uncomfortable for informal migrant entrepreneurs. On World Refugee Day in June, SAPS and military officers, traffic officials, Metro police and immigration officials descended en masse on the Cape Town Station Deck, a well-known taxi terminus and market above the Cape Town railway station.[2] They closed it for four hours and raided all the stalls, later trumpeting the arrest of 81 "foreign nationals" and the confiscation of ZAR150,000 in "counterfeit goods" and "substantial amounts" of dagga. The perspective of the informal traders on what happened was less triumphal:

> *Yesterday was a big loss. We had prepared food that could not be delivered to our customers as usual. No one was allowed to come in or out of the deck. Soldiers and police had blocked all entrances and exit points. I have not yet paid my workers…Since I started this business (selling pap and mutton stew) in 2010, I never let my workers down when it comes to paying wages.*[3]

> *The police, they come to the shop next door all the time, and they get nothing. It's a Nigerian shop, and each and every time they search they find nothing, but they still come back. When they came Saturday, they went next door and they*

said they heard that shop is open 24/7. We pay rent; it's none of their business if we open 24/7, and the way we are paying the rent, they don't give us choice… you must make money the way you know how, which is to open 24/7. After they search the shop, they turn the shop upside down. They leave it just like that, and they said: "It's not the last time you will see me in this shop."[4]

They asked me for my document. I take my passport and showed them, and they left. I've been here for five years already. Nothing like this has happened to me. Most of the people didn't have their documents (with them), and there was nowhere to run – it was all over the place. I saw they arrested a woman, but she was back here yesterday. She didn't have her document on Saturday, but she maybe asked her kids to bring it to the police so she could be released. The army thing, I don't understand why they are here. They carry those guns like it's war here. If you come to search the people like that, it's not good, because even today some shops didn't open because the people were worried about that.[5]

I didn't know what was happening. I just came to the train station and when I came upstairs, everything was closed. The police told us that we can't enter. There were many people: police, army, and law enforcement. Downstairs there was nothing, they didn't ask anyone about papers. I have my papers, but my papers are expired. If they saw my documents that day, they would arrest me. I didn't renew them, because people say that to go to Home Affairs you must pay R2,000 to make the new documents. You need money and I don't have money. It makes you feel pain, because they arrest you and they take you away, and you don't want to go. There's no jobs in Malawi. My friend, she works here, and she was arrested. I spoke to her on the phone – I asked her where she is; she said she's by the police but she don't know which police station. She say she don't know anything. When I tried again later, her phone was on voicemail.[6]

It was really terrifying the manner in which they did [things] yesterday. Soldiers pointed guns, ready to shoot anyone [who was] against what was happening. I was selling some brand stuff, but these people went beyond that. Some of them were wicked. I could neither question their authority nor do anything to stop them from taking my stuff. They came in and took down all my stuff. They confiscated almost 50 items [including] jeans, trousers and tops. Out of these items, less than 10 were brand names. Yesterday was a great loss, since *the operation went into our busiest time of the day, between 10 and 11am… The unfortunate thing is they did not give us a receipt to show what they have confiscated… I believe in a normal situation they issue a receipt… We did not get any chance to talk to them regarding how we could go about [getting back] the goods seized.*[7]

The contrast between the Mayor's welcoming words and events on the streets of Cape Town could not be starker, especially when it comes to the treatment of informal entrepreneurs from other countries. Threats of violence and actual attacks on migrant entrepreneurs and their properties by South African rivals and ordinary citizens are a common phenomenon throughout the city.[8] In 2008, during an upsurge of attacks on migrant-owned businesses, about 200 Somali businessmen in Western Cape province were threatened with violence if they continued doing business in the townships. A group of local township businessmen, under the banner of the Zanokhanyo Retailers' Association, sent letters to the Somalis, warning them to close their shops or face "actions that will include physically fighting."[9] The Somali Community Board claims that over 400 Somalis, many of them informal traders, were murdered in South Africa between early 2002 and mid-2010.[10] Business robberies often result in deaths or serious injuries; Somalis interviewed in one study "were most traumatised by crimes orchestrated against them by South African traders, including assassination style killings and arson attacks that resulted in some Somali traders being burnt to death."[11] The police are frequently accused of fomenting or turning a blind eye to xenophobic attacks on migrant businesses. Whether true or not, there is little evidence that the attackers are ever arrested or convicted. One study reports that police collude in restricting the numbers of migrant entrepreneurs operating in townships.[12]

## RESEARCH METHODOLOGY

Studies of the "hidden" role of migrant informal entrepreneurship in Cape Town have begun to proliferate.[13] This report builds on this research with the largest survey yet of African migrant and refugee entrepreneurs from over 20 countries in different parts of the city. Here we discuss the research design, which combined qualitative and quantitative methods to provide a better understanding of the origins, operations, opportunities, and problems confronting migrant entrepreneurs. The quantitative component of the study involved the administration of the standardized SAMP-GIC questionnaire to a sample of migrant entrepreneurs. The questionnaire sought information on the origin of the enterprises, their ownership, structure, capitalization, income, growth, and employment creation potential as well as problems they faced. Qualitative data collection entailed the use of in-depth interviews, key informant interviews, and focus group discussions. The survey and interviews generated information on the links between international migration and informality, the opportunities available to the entrepreneurs to grow their businesses, and the obstacles they face in their business operations.

The SAMP-GIC questionnaire was administered to a sample of 518 migrant owners of micro-enterprises in Cape Town by graduate research assistants drawn from the University of Cape Town (UCT) and the Cape Peninsula University of Technology (CPUT). The micro-enterprises had to meet all three basic criteria for inclusion: (a) owned by a non-South African; (b) in operation for at least two years to allow for a retrospective analysis of the start-up, problems, and opportunities; and (c) unregistered with the South African Revenue Services (SARS). The questionnaires were administered in four areas that were purposively selected: Imizamo Yethu, Philippi, Bellville, and Cape Town CBD (Table 1). Although migrant entrepreneurs are located in most areas of the city, these areas have particular concentrations of migrant-owned businesses.

Table 1: Geographical Distribution of Survey Sample

|  | No. | % |
| --- | --- | --- |
| Imizamo Yethu | 103 | 19.9 |
| Philippi | 106 | 20.5 |
| Bellville | 154 | 29.7 |
| CBD | 155 | 29.9 |
| Total | 518 | 100.0 |

In all the survey areas, systematic random sampling was used. As almost all micro-enterprises were located at street level, every third enterprise along a street was selected. The starting point in each area was established by identifying the first six enterprises, assigning numbers to them and then rolling a dice to pick the starting point. Thereafter, every third enterprise was selected. Should the selected enterprise belong to a South African citizen or not meet all three criteria, it was substituted by the next one and the process was repeated until a street was covered.

A total of 30 in-depth interviews were conducted with selected owners of informal micro-enterprises. The selection of respondents occurred during the questionnaire administration phase when all were asked if they were willing to partake in an in-depth interview. A semi-structured interview schedule was used for the interviews. This allowed the interviewers to probe for additional information by pursuing interesting issues through follow-up questions. Twenty two of the 30 in-depth interviews were recorded and later transcribed for use. The responses of the other eight were captured through note-taking. Two focus group discussions were held in the Cape Town CBD and Philippi respectively. The former had seven participants and the latter six. The aim of the focus groups was to elicit more in-depth information on the perceptions, insights, attitudes, and experiences of migrant entrepreneurs regarding their involvement in the informal sector, the opportunities they saw, the problems and hurdles they faced and the institutional mechanisms and regulations governing their operation in the city. The size of the two focus groups was manageable and each lasted for about 100 minutes.

Fifteen key informant interviews were held with various stakeholders in Cape Town to understand the operation and constraints faced by migrants operating in the informal economy. These included the City of Cape Town, the Department of Trade and Industry, and the Small Enterprise Development Agency, as well as some diaspora organizations. The selection of key informants was based on their ability to supply information relevant to the migrant enterprises and general issues regarding the operation of micro-enterprises.

## PROFILE OF INFORMAL MIGRANT ENTREPRENEURS

The age profile of the interviewed migrants varied considerably from a minimum of 18 to a maximum of 62 years. Most were relatively young, however, with 23% aged between 25 and 29 and 27% between 30 and 34. In total, nearly 80% of the sample was aged below 40 (Figure 1). The general youthfulness of the entrepreneurs is both a reflection of the tendency for migrants to South Africa to be working-age adults and the fact that informal business activity generally requires one to be physically fit enough to haul large loads of goods to and from storerooms to the street on a daily basis, to brave unfavourable weather conditions in the open, and sometimes to engage in running battles with municipal police. Men outnumbered women by 73% to 27%.

Figure 1: Age of Survey Respondents

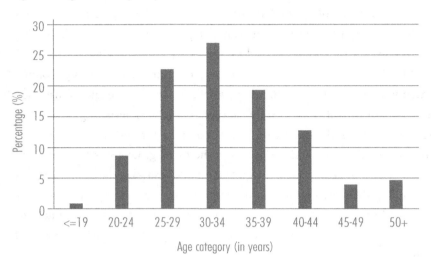

Age category (in years)

The sample was relatively educated in comparison with the South African population, although the numbers with post-secondary education were not large. Only 4% indicated that they had no formal education (Table 2). Most of the respondents (89%) had some secondary education: 36% had completed secondary or high school and another 28% had some secondary education. Around 17% held a college certificate or diploma, 6% had some university education, and 2% had completed an undergraduate degree.

Table 2: Educational Levels of Migrant Entrepreneurs and South Africans

|  | Migrant entrepreneurs (%) | South Africans (%) (Census 2011) |
|---|---|---|
| No formal schooling | 3.9 | 8.6 |
| Primary only | 5.7 | 16.9 |
| Some secondary | 27.6 | 33.9 |
| Secondary/high school diploma | 36.0 | 28.9 |
| Post-secondary qualifications | 25.6 | 11.8 |
| Other | 1.2 | 0.0 |
| Total | 100.0 | 100.0 |

The migrant entrepreneurs came predominantly from Zimbabwe, Somalia, the DRC, Nigeria, Malawi, Ethiopia and Cameroon (Table 3). Just over a third (36%) were from other SADC countries. The prominence of Zimbabwean entrepreneurs in the Cape Town informal economy is not surprising, given the negative events in that country over the past decade and a half and the resultant mass migration to South Africa.[14] A total of 57% of the entrepreneurs were from other African countries, especially the DRC, Somalia, Nigeria and Ethiopia. The majority of migrants from these countries (with the exception of Nigeria) would have come to South Africa as refugees. The political crisis in Somalia over the past two decades has seen an influx of migrants into South Africa, where most seek and are granted asylum.[15]

Table 3: Country of Origin of Migrant Entrepreneurs

|  | No. | % |
|---|---|---|
| **SADC** | | |
| Zimbabwe | 118 | 22.8 |
| Malawi | 39 | 7.5 |
| Tanzania | 9 | 1.7 |
| Lesotho | 5 | 1.0 |
| Zambia | 5 | 1.0 |
| Angola | 4 | 0.8 |
| Mozambique | 4 | 0.8 |
| **Other African** | | |
| Somalia | 70 | 13.5 |
| Democratic Republic of the Congo | 58 | 11.2 |
| Nigeria | 48 | 9.3 |
| Ethiopia | 37 | 7.2 |
| Cameroon | 22 | 4.3 |
| Ghana | 17 | 3.3 |
| Congo (Brazzaville) | 14 | 2.7 |
| Uganda | 12 | 2.3 |
| Kenya | 11 | 2.1 |
| Rwanda | 5 | 1.0 |

| Other | | |
|---|---|---|
| Pakistan | 8 | 1.5 |
| Bangladesh | 4 | 0.8 |
| Other country | 27 | 5.2 |
| Total | 517 | 100.0 |

Migrants generally have more than one reason for migrating. In an effort to capture this multi-faceted aspect, the survey asked the respondents to rate several different possible motives in terms of their level of importance. Wanting to provide for their families back home was cited as an important factor by 72%, closely followed by those who came to the country to seek asylum (68%) (Figure 2). As many as 62% said they came with the intention of starting a business. At the same time, 48% said they came to look for employment, which suggests that some entrepreneurs may have been rationalizing their later decision to become an entrepreneur as their original intention for coming. The responses also provide insights into the role of migrant networks: while only 18% said they had originally come to join a family business, as many as 47% said they had been encouraged to come to South Africa by friends and relatives.

Figure 2: Reasons for Migrating to South Africa

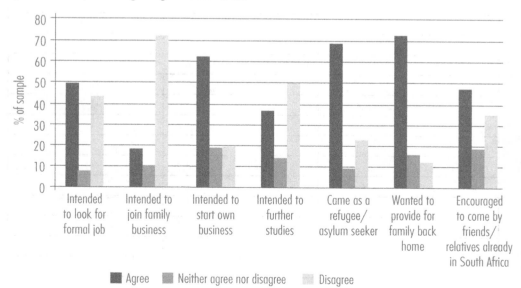

Just under a third of the migrant entrepreneurs had refugee permits (Table 4). Of these, 59% came from only three countries: the DRC, Ethiopia and Somalia. A further 31% held asylum-seeker permits. Of these, 32% were Zimbabwean while a significant number came from the DRC, Ethiopia and Somalia (another 30% in total). However, only a few Zimbabweans have ever been granted refugee status because South Africa maintains that Zimbabweans are not political refugees but economic migrants.[16] Nearly 12% had permanent residence permits while 8% had work permits. Zimbabweans held more than half (53%) of the work permits, mostly obtained through the Zimbabwean Dispensation Project implemented by the South African government in late 2010.[17] Only 7% of the respondents indicated that they did not have official documentation to stay in South Africa. More importantly, the profile drawn from this research shows that the vast majority of migrant entrepreneurs are in fact forced migrants who deserve protection under international and South African refugee law. Rather than being victimized for choosing to enter the informal economy, they deserve greater protection from the state as they seek to rebuild their lives in a foreign land.

Table 4: Immigration Status of Migrant Entrepreneurs

|  | No. | % |
| --- | --- | --- |
| Refugee permit holder | 162 | 31.5 |
| Asylum-seeker permit holder | 158 | 30.7 |
| Permanent resident of South Africa | 61 | 11.9 |
| Work permit holder | 40 | 7.8 |
| No official documentation | 38 | 7.4 |
| Visitor's permit holder | 30 | 5.8 |
| Other immigration status | 12 | 2.3 |
| Refused/No answer | 12 | 2.4 |
| Citizen of South Africa | 1 | 0.2 |
| Total | 514 | 100.0 |

## MOVING TO SOUTH AFRICA

Very few of the migrant entrepreneurs had entered South Africa before 1994 and only 8% had arrived in the immediate post-apartheid years. While another 20% came between 2000 and 2004, the vast majority (70%) arrived during the last decade: as many as 44% between 2005 and 2009 and a further 27% thereafter (Table 5). Migration from Zimbabwe certainly escalated between 2005 and 2009 as the country plunged deeper into crisis. It is also possible that South Africa's nationwide xenophobic violence in 2008 and continuing attacks on migrant businesses have exercised a dampening effect on migration and discouraged migrant entrepreneurship in recent years.[18]

Table 5: Year of Arrival in South Africa

|  | No. | % |
|---|---|---|
| Before 1994 | 2 | 0.4 |
| 1994-1999 | 43 | 8.4 |
| 2000-2004 | 106 | 20.5 |
| 2005-2009 | 226 | 43.7 |
| 2010-2014 | 140 | 27.1 |
| Total | 517 | 100.0 |

Despite the perception that unemployment at home is a driver of migration, only 14% of the entrepreneurs were unemployed immediately before leaving for South Africa (Table 6). Another 19% were students, which means that around two-thirds were engaged in some form of income-generating activity before leaving or being forced to leave. Twenty-six percent were working in the informal economy in their home countries, while the rest (40%) were working in the formal economy as skilled and unskilled manual workers, professionals, farm workers, office workers, teachers, domestic workers, and in a range of other jobs. Some respondents were involved in more than one activity; for example, holding a job and running an informal business at the same time.

When migrants move to South Africa, they are rarely guaranteed the same types of jobs they had back home. Being in a new environment with its own labour market and demands, many migrants struggle to find suitable employment and are forced to accept low-paying jobs. Around 60% had worked in the formal sector since coming to South Africa, primarily as unskilled manual workers (20%), skilled manual workers (11%), domestic workers (10%), farm workers (6%) and security workers (5%) (Table 7). Only 12% had experienced periods of unemployment and 7% had been students. Some had started informal businesses while still at school to help finance their studies, while others started their business after finishing their education and failing to find formal employment. As many as 56% had operated a different business from the one they were currently operating, either doing the same (41%) or a different activity (15%).

Table 6: Occupation before Leaving Home Country

|  | No. | % |
|---|---|---|
| Operated own informal sector business | 152 | 36.1 |
| Scholar/student | 112 | 19.3 |
| Unemployed | 80 | 13.8 |
| Skilled manual worker | 35 | 6.0 |
| Professional (e.g. lawyer, doctor, academic, engineer) | 32 | 5.5 |
| Agricultural worker | 32 | 5.5 |
| Unskilled manual worker | 29 | 5.0 |
| Office worker | 26 | 4.5 |
| Teacher | 12 | 2.1 |
| Police/military/security | 10 | 1.7 |
| Domestic worker | 10 | 1.7 |
| Formal sector business owner | 4 | 0.7 |
| Employer/manager | 3 | 0.5 |
| Mineworker | 2 | 0.3 |
| Health worker | 1 | 0.2 |
| Other occupation | 33 | 5.7 |
| Total | 563 | 100.0 |

Table 7: Occupations since Migrating to South Africa

|  | No. | % of total |
|---|---|---|
| **Business** | | |
| Operated informal business (same activity as now) | 211 | 40.7 |
| Operated informal business (different activity than now) | 77 | 14.9 |
| Businessman/woman formal sector (self-employed) | 10 | 1.9 |
| **Employment** | | |
| Unskilled manual worker | 104 | 20.0 |
| Skilled manual worker | 57 | 11.0 |
| Domestic worker | 50 | 9.7 |
| Farm worker | 31 | 6.0 |
| Security | 26 | 5.0 |

| Professional | 18 | 3.5 |
|---|---|---|
| Office worker | 15 | 2.9 |
| Teacher | 5 | 1.0 |
| Mineworker | 2 | 0.4 |
| Employer/manager | 1 | 0.2 |
| Health worker | 1 | 0.2 |
| **Other** | | |
| Unemployed | 64 | 8.2 |
| Other occupation | 56 | 7.2 |
| Student | 35 | 4.5 |
| Total | 763 | 100.0 |
| Note: multiple response question | | |

## ENTREPRENEURIAL MOTIVATION

Research in South Africa has shown that migrants, especially refugees, face many barriers in gaining access to formal employment leading many to find work in the informal economy.[19] The possibilities for informal entrepreneurship are mediated by several factors, including the ease of acquisition of relevant skills. For instance, if the skills required for a certain entrepreneurial activity can only be acquired through training programmes, individuals who do not have access to such programmes face barriers of entry. The survey sought to investigate how migrant entrepreneurs in Cape Town acquired the skills that they used in their business. Many cited more than one method of acquiring the relevant skills. The majority (64%) said that they were self-taught while 44% said they had learned skills from friends and relatives (Table 8). Around a quarter (26%) had acquired skills from previous work experience (26%). The number with formal business skills training was much lower: 8% had training from a university, school or training centre; 7% had accessed a government training course; and 3% had training from NGOs. A total of 11% said they did not need any particular skills in their business. In total, less than 10% had formal training to help them acquire the skills used in their business activity.

Table 8: Method of Acquiring Skills Used in Business

| | No. | % of total |
|---|---|---|
| **Informal** | | |
| Self-taught | 332 | 64.1 |
| Learning from friends and relatives | 227 | 43.8 |
| Previous work experience | 136 | 26.4 |
| Apprenticeship/on the job training | 57 | 11.0 |
| **Formal** | | |
| University, school or other training centre | 44 | 8.5 |
| Training courses/programmes (government) | 37 | 7.1 |
| Training courses/ programmes (NGO, private sector) | 18 | 3.5 |
| **Other** | | |
| Other methods | 6 | 1.1 |
| No skills needed | 55 | 10.6 |
| Note: multiple response question | | |

Are entrepreneurs born or made? This question has spawned a large literature examining whether entrepreneurs have a natural predisposition towards entrepreneurship in terms of personal motivation and orientation.[20] Some argue that examining the reasons why people establish businesses is useful in understanding entrepreneurial motivation and orientation. The current study therefore examined the factors that motivated migrants in Cape Town to establish a business. In general terms, these can be classified as pull and push factors. Push factors that drive migrants into entrepreneurship relate mostly to employment factors. On the other hand, pull factors include monetary or financial motivations, the desire for prestige or independence, intrinsic rewards (that is, self-fulfilment and growth) and various other human, social and economic factors.

To identify these "entrepreneurial triggers", respondents were asked to rank the importance of various factors on a motivation scale ranging from 1 (no importance) to 5 (extremely important). Table 9 presents the results of this exercise in the form of a mean score for the respondents as a whole on each of the 24 factors that were pre-identified as components of entrepreneurial motivation. Each of these factors was grouped into one of four general categories: financial benefits and security; entrepreneurial orientation and personal rewards; building social capital; and creating employment. Of these, creating employment scored the lowest with all factors scoring less than 3.0. In other words, unemployment and the desire to provide employment for others did not rate particularly highly as motives for entrepreneurship. Insofar as employment creation was a factor, it is of interest that creating jobs for family and for South Africans both scored 2.5 (and better than creating jobs for other people from the home country at 2.2).

Within the group of factors relating to *building social capital*, there was considerable diversity with four factors scoring over 3.0 and three less than 2.5. Less important were factors relating to working collaboratively to establish a business. More significant were the desire to provide a product or service to South Africans (3.9) and other immigrants (3.7) and a desire to contribute to the development of South Africa (3.6). In general, it was personal motivations and rewards (as in the financial benefits and security group and the intrinsic rewards group) that consistently scored the highest with every factor rating over 3.0. The highest scoring was in the *entrepreneurial orientation and personal rewards* category and included "being one's own boss" (at 4.1 the highest mean score overall), having the right personality to run a business (3.9) and a desire to challenge oneself (3.8). Overall, this suggests that the migrant entrepreneurs tended to go into business because they felt that they were personally suited to this kind of activity as independent-minded people looking for a challenge, wanting to learn new skills and willing to take risks.

At the same time, material factors cannot be entirely discounted as the scores in the *financial benefits and security* category were also high. The highest factor of all was needing more money to survive (4.1). Other material motivations included greater financial security for the family (3.9) and making money to remit to the home country (3.8). Another high-scoring factor was the long-term desire to run their own business (at 4.0), which can also be seen as another sign of independence and intrinsic reward. However, while the entrepreneurs tend to favour individualistic explanations for why they established their business, when it comes to the economic fruits of that business, they tend to take a more social stance, emphasizing the benefits to family in South Africa and, through remittances, their home country.

In sum, while financial factors provided the strongest motivation to start a business, it was also a means of fulfilling personal goals and aspirations. For others, entrepreneurship provided them with a way of serving the community, including South Africans, their own families, and the wider immigrant community in South Africa. Therefore, the success of immigrant-owned businesses does not only result in individual benefits accruing to the entrepreneurs but the benefits are likely to be felt by the general population including ordinary South Africans and other migrants.

Table 9: The Motivation to Start a Business

| Factor | Mean score |
|---|---|
| **Financial benefits/security** | |
| I needed more money just to survive | 4.1 |
| I have always wanted to run my own business | 4.0 |
| I wanted to give my family greater financial security | 3.9 |
| I wanted to make more money to send to my family in my home country | 3.8 |
| **Entrepreneurial orientation and personal rewards** | |
| I wanted more control over my own time/to be my own boss | 4.1 |
| I have the right personality to run my own business | 3.9 |
| I like to challenge myself | 3.8 |
| I like to learn new skills | 3.7 |
| I enjoy taking risks | 3.6 |
| I wanted to do something new and challenging | 3.5 |
| I wanted to compete with others and be the best | 3.3 |
| **Building social capital** | |
| I wanted to provide a product/service to South Africans | 3.9 |
| I wanted to contribute to the development of South Africa | 3.6 |
| I had a good idea for a service/product for other immigrants | 3.7 |
| I wanted to increase my status in the community | 3.2 |
| Support and help in starting my business was available from other immigrants | 2.4 |
| My family members have always been involved in business | 2.2 |
| I decided to go into business in partnership with others | 2.1 |
| **Creating employment** | |
| I was unemployed and unable to find a job | 2.9 |
| I wanted to provide employment for members of my family | 2.5 |
| I wanted to provide employment for South Africans | 2.5 |
| I had a job but it did not pay enough | 2.4 |
| I wanted to provide employment for other people from my home country | 2.2 |
| I had a job but it did not suit my qualifications and experience | 2.0 |

## BUSINESS OWNERSHIP AND STRATEGIES

The survey collected detailed information about the entrepreneurs' businesses on issues such as the year of establishment, who started the business, the amount and source of start-up capital, and the current value of the business. The survey concentrated on micro-enterprises in three major sectors: (a) retail, trade and wholesale; (b) manufacturing; and (c) services. About 62% of the migrant entrepreneurs were engaged in retail, trade and wholesale activities, 28% in services, and 10% in manufacturing (Figure 3). A number of entrepreneurs were engaged in more than one sector; for example, manufacturing crafts as well as selling shoes.

Figure 3: Sectoral Breakdown of Migrant Businesses

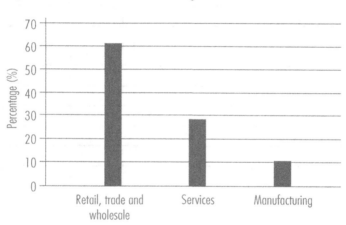

The entrepreneurs conducted their business activities from a variety of temporary and permanent locations (Table 10). Some, particularly the more mobile, operated in more than one location. The most significant location was a temporary stall on the street (38% of the total sample). Next was a permanent stall on the street (at 21%). Other fixed premises included workshops or shops (16%), their own home (11%), a permanent stall in a market (11%) and a shop in a house, yard or garage (3%). Other temporary sites of significance included taxi ranks (11%) and in the customer's home (3%). A total of 9% were mobile, predominantly selling goods door to door.

Table 10: Location Where Business Usually Conducted

| | No. | % of total |
|---|---|---|
| **Permanent** | | |
| Permanent stall on the street | 109 | 21.0 |
| Workshop or shop | 85 | 16.4 |
| Permanent stall in a market | 55 | 10.6 |
| In own home | 55 | 10.6 |
| Shop in house/yard/garage | 18 | 3.5 |
| Taxi/public transport station in permanent structure | 10 | 1.9 |
| Restaurant or hotel | 2 | 0.4 |
| **Temporary** | | |
| Temporary stall on the street | 198 | 38.2 |
| Taxi rank | 57 | 11.0 |
| Mobile (e.g. door to door) | 46 | 8.9 |
| In customer's home (e.g. hairstyling) | 17 | 3.3 |
| From vehicle (car, truck, motor bike, bike) | 6 | 1.2 |
| **Other** | | |
| Other location | 34 | 6.6 |
| N | 518 | |
| Note: multiple response question | | |

Only a few of the businesses (less than 5%) were established before 2000. The majority (over 50%) started between 2010 and 2014 (Figure 4). In general, the data suggests that the rapid growth of non-South Africans in the city's informal economy is a relatively recent phenomenon and may account, in part, for the growing hostility that migrant entrepreneurs are facing. Comparing the year in which the migrant came to South Africa with the year they established their business shows that there is a clear time lag between the two. In other words, most migrants do not establish a business as soon as they arrive.

Over 70% of the migrants started their business on their own, without the assistance of others. This is consistent with the findings about individualism in the analysis of entrepreneurial motivation above (Table 11). Only 15% started the business with other migrants from their home countries, and 12% with members of their family. Only 4% reported starting with South African partners. Even fewer took over businesses that had been started by South Africans.

Figure 4: Year of Arrival and Year of Business Establishment

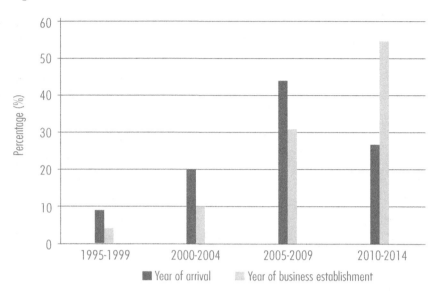

Table 11: Origins of Business

|  | No. | % of total |
| --- | --- | --- |
| I started it alone | 371 | 71.6 |
| I started it with people from my home country | 77 | 14.9 |
| I started it with my family | 65 | 12.5 |
| I started it with people from other countries | 22 | 4.2 |
| I started it with South African business partners | 11 | 2.1 |
| I bought this business from a non-South African | 8 | 1.5 |
| I bought this business from a South African | 5 | 1.0 |
| Other | 3 | 0.6 |
| N | 518 |  |
| Note: multiple response question | | |

A key issue confronting small businesses in general, and informal businesses in particular, is the perception that they have low profit margins, a high rate of failure and do not grow. Such perceptions stem from the argument that the driving force behind most of these establishments is mere survival. One question that this study sought to answer was whether the businesses operated by migrant entrepreneurs are survivalist enterprises on the periphery of the economy or vibrant enterprises capable of increasing their capitalization. The study therefore collected data on the sources and amounts of start-up capital used to establish the business and the current value of the business. Differences between the start-up and the current value of a business provide evidence of growth or contraction of the enterprise.

Obtaining start-up business capital can be a daunting exercise for migrants and refugees in South Africa. They frequently lack the necessary collateral to acquire a loan from financial institutions. Various reasons were provided for why banks turned down loan applications. The most common was that the migrants were "not South African" and did not have identity documents, an indictment of the banks given how many of the entrepreneurs have a legal right to be in South Africa. Others were turned down because their enterprise was deemed unviable by a bank. Still others were rejected on the basis that they lacked collateral and had insufficient operating capital.

Unsurprisingly, therefore, the vast majority of migrant entrepreneurs (81%) used personal savings to start the business (Table 12). Most self-financing migrants used savings from prior employment:

> We came without any money. But from small piece work jobs we did here and there, my friend and I were able to save some money and obtain a certain capital that allowed us to start something informal. God helped us to find a place where we could expose our business to meet clients.[21]

> The secret of business capital is to save little by little because there is nowhere you can get money. I started by saving little by little until I had something big enough to start something consistent. So I started very small. I kept on saving and increasing the quantity of my products until I became like this. As for others, I think they get help from their families. But there is no one who just gets free money.[22]

> Our work does not need capital. The first thing is your own energy and skill. If you have no money you can borrow. It always begins like I am doing now. You first work for someone else. After some years, I can decide to have my own activity. So you can find help or you need to help yourself. But the bank is not for us. We help each other instead.[23]

Other sources of start-up funds were loans from relatives (29%) and non-relatives, usually other migrants from their home country (16%). The use of both formal and informal financial institutions was limited, which emphasizes self-reliance and personal networks as sources of business start-up capital. As one female entrepreneur observed:

> I started with a few thousand rands from my friends and relatives. I pay them back little by little and they understand. That is how we do it. Others they come with their own money to start a business, but those are the few. Most of us we came with very little and so we borrow or we work for others until we raise the money to start on our own. It's wasting time to go to the bank. Once they see you and you cannot produce an ID, then they say we cannot help.[24]

Table 12: Primary Sources of Start-up Capital

| | No. | % of total |
|---|---|---|
| Personal savings | 418 | 81.6 |
| Loan from relatives | 149 | 29.1 |
| Loan from non-relatives | 81 | 15.8 |
| Money lenders | 9 | 1.8 |
| Loan from informal financial institutions | 7 | 1.4 |
| Business credit (goods on terms) | 5 | 1.0 |
| Loan from micro-finance institution | 1 | 0.2 |
| Other source of capital | 23 | 4.5 |
| N | 512 | |
| Note: multiple response question | | |

Once a business is established, very few of the entrepreneurs seek loans. The majority (83%) had not acquired a single loan in the previous 12 months. While 28% had obtained loans from relatives in the start-up phase, only 9% had done so in the previous year. Only a tiny minority (less than 3%) had ever obtained loans from other formal and informal sources (Table 13). Only 18 individuals (or 3.5%) of the sample had tried to apply for a bank loan. Of these, only 5 (or 1%) had managed to secure loans. What this indicates is that the growth of a business is entirely dependent on the reinvestment of profits from that business. While migrant entrepreneurs receive no assistance from South African banks, they are also unable to access government support schemes for small-scale businesses. Only 1% of the respondents had benefited from such schemes.

Table 13: Source of Business Loans

|  | No. | % of total |
|---|---|---|
| Loan from relatives | 49 | 9.4 |
| Loan from other business owners | 27 | 5.2 |
| Business credit (goods on terms) | 9 | 1.7 |
| *Mashonisa* (money lenders) | 6 | 1.1 |
| Loan from banks | 5 | 1.0 |
| Informal financial institution | 3 | 0.6 |
| Micro-finance institution | 2 | 0.4 |
| Other source of loan | 7 | 1.3 |
| N | 518 |  |
| Note: multiple response question | | |

The question, then, is whether businesses are able to grow despite the absence of credit and lack of government support. The survey found that while more than two-thirds of the sample had less than ZAR10,000 to start their business, only 23% valued their current business at less than ZAR10,000 (Figure 5). On the other hand, while only 7% had at least ZAR30,000 at start-up, nearly 30% valued their current business at more than ZAR30,000, suggesting an upward trend in the value of migrant-owned enterprises in the Cape Town area. This is further evidence that informal migrant entrepreneurship is more than just survivalist; a great many of the entrepreneurs have managed to scale up their business operations.

On average the respondents earn profits of ZAR4,121 per month or approximately ZAR50,000 per year from their business activities. This is less than the ZAR60,613 average income for black families in South Africa recorded in the 2011 census (Statistics South Africa, 2012). However, the latter includes many middle-class families with much higher incomes. As many as 15% earn more than ZAR6,000 per month from their business activities (Figure 6).

Figure 5: Comparison between Start-up Capital and Current Business Value

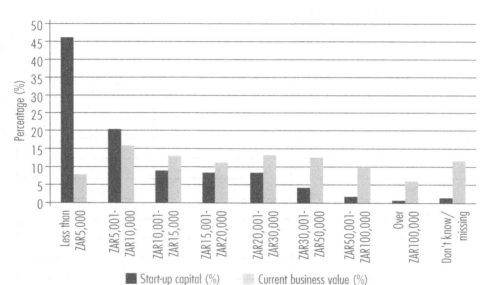

Figure 6: Monthly Profit from Business Activities

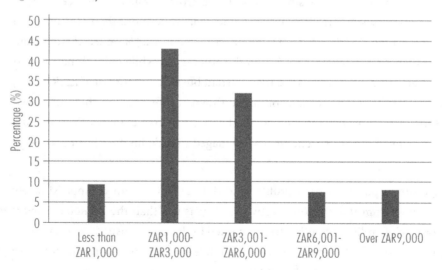

# CONTRIBUTIONS TO THE CAPE TOWN ECONOMY

Migrants have long been portrayed by officials, citizens and the media as having a negative impact on the South African economy and undermining the livelihoods of South Africans. The prevalence of such perceptions helps to explain growing xenophobic sentiment against migrants and refugees.[25] Contrary to these popular perceptions, an emerging literature on migrant entrepreneurship is beginning to demonstrate the positive economic contributions of migrants.[26]

This project sought to establish the contribution of migrant entrepreneurs to the local economy using three main indicators: paying rent, purchasing arrangements, and employment of South Africans. First, with regard to rent, over a third of the respondents (34%) pay rent to the city council or municipality (Table 14). Furthermore, 31% pay rent to the South African private owner of their business premises and 9% to a non-South African private owner. This means that the majority of entrepreneurs, despite being in the informal economy, pay rent to the local government and/or South African property owners. Only a quarter of the respondents said they did not pay any rent. A small minority (14%) were the owners or part-owners of their business premises. The average rent paid per month varied widely with a mean monthly rental of ZAR2,223. Some of the rents were clearly exorbitant and were negatively affecting the job-creation potential of the business:

> The problem here is rentals. It is expensive. It is a company that changes management. Sometimes they put in someone who comes with changes in the rentals. Like recently, we signed a contract for three years and rentals went up and up. There used to be many people working with me but they are not here any more because of rent. Sometimes you can only make enough money for rent and don't benefit.[27]

> The cost of living is high, the rent is expensive where I am staying in Cape Town. I am paying R1,800 per month. And the shop I am renting here is R11,000 per month. The only trouble here is just the rent. If the government can do something about this, we will be very thankful and grateful. The rent is killing us. It is stressing us a lot. The rents are just too high.[28]

> This place used to be a packing place for vehicles. We negotiated with the owner and changed it into a market place and we pay rent. So everyone has a responsibility to pay rent, or else there is no market here. You cannot conduct

*business here if you don't have money. So we pay R30,000 for this place. Sometimes a few of us are forced to pay all that money to keep the place. If we are still here it is because we pay every time. We would not be here if we failed to pay a month. Others come from Greenmarket [Square] and store their luggage here and pay about R800 monthly.*[29]

In total, the respondents collectively paid a mean monthly rent of ZAR805,000 or ZAR9.7 million per year.

Table 14: Occupancy/Tenure Status of Business Premises

|  | No. | % of total |
|---|---|---|
| Pay rent to council/ municipality | 177 | 34.2 |
| Pay rent to private owner who is a South African | 162 | 31.3 |
| Rent-free, with permission | 98 | 18.9 |
| I own it/am part owner | 72 | 13.9 |
| Rent-free, without permission (squatting) | 47 | 9.1 |
| Pay rent to private owner who is not South African | 45 | 8.7 |
| Other occupancy/tenure status | 8 | 1.5 |
| Note: multiple response question | | |

Some entrepreneurs rent larger business spaces from South African owners and then sub-let on a regular or occasional basis to vendors who supply wholesale goods to other vendors:

*The people selling here are small business people from various places such as Zimbabwe, Malawi, Namibia and Tanzania. This is a wholesale market. The people out there come to order from here. So we created this place as a platform for people coming from various places to expose their products here. When they come, we give them a small space. They sell their products and go back home and others come in. Every day there are those that come in and those that leave. They pay something to us and we also pay to the owner of the place.*[30]

Second, purchasing agreements are another way in which to gauge the migrant contribution to the local economy. If, for example, migrant entrepreneurs sourced their commodities locally this would help spur local economic development. A large number of respondents indicated that they sourced their goods locally from wholesalers (63%), small shops and retailers (20%), supermarkets (15%) and from factories (15%) (Table 15). A smaller number (11%) sourced produce (mainly fruit and vegetables) from the Epping fresh produce market. Only a small proportion sourced the goods from another country (10%) or their home country (7%).

A common accusation levelled by South African informal sector entrepreneurs against migrants is that they frequently engage in group buying, pooling their resources with other entrepreneurs and negotiating better deals with wholesalers and manufacturers. This is a perfectly legal practice which, lest it be forgotten, directly translates into lower prices for consumers. Such group-buying practices have been documented in several studies.[31] On the other hand, some studies have contested whether the practice exists, arguing instead that migrants do not buy in groups but are very attuned to price differences at various outlets.[32] The present study found that group buying in bulk did exist but was far from universal. Just over a third of the respondents (36%) engaged in this practice. This means that nearly two-thirds of our sample did not.

Given that many of the respondents source their goods from wholesalers, who usually sell in bulk, it makes sense for small entrepreneurs to combine into groups to benefit from buying in bulk. One wholesaler interviewed for this project said that, in his experience, Somalis were the most adept at group buying and that very few South Africans engaged in the practice. He noted that, in the early stages, small businesses get together to form a "buying corporation" or "buying group":

> They buy together to get better prices by buying in bulk. Instead of buying one case and getting a price for 10, they'll buy 20 because they'll get a better price. They will elect a committee, two or three of them and they will do the buying. Some of them have little warehouses. They will buy the stock into the warehouse and redistribute to themselves by a little bakkie (small truck) to each shop. That's how they deal with it. It's not 20 of them all of a sudden. If they belong to a buying group they elect somebody to represent them, and that person will come and do the buying and it's normally their best negotiator.[33]

Buying groups normally comprise a group of start-ups and once individuals have grown their businesses sufficiently to buy in bulk on their own, they opt out of a buying group.

Third, migrant entrepreneurs create jobs in Cape Town in three main ways. First, by buying goods from retailers and wholesalers they directly support the employees of South African-based manufacturers who sell their goods through the local retailers and wholesalers. Second, they support local jobs at the wholesalers and retailers where they buy their goods. Third, they play an important role in direct hiring of people to work for them in their businesses. While other studies have documented the extent to which migrants create employment and opportunities for fellow immigrants, especially those from their home country, less is known about the full range of opportunities that they create for all people, including South Africans.[34]

Table 15: Source of Goods and Supplies

| | No. | % of total |
|---|---|---|
| **Suppliers** | | |
| Wholesalers | 329 | 63.5 |
| Small shops/retailers | 102 | 19.7 |
| Supermarkets | 77 | 14.9 |
| Direct from factory | 76 | 14.7 |
| Epping fresh produce market | 57 | 11.0 |
| Direct from farmers | 14 | 2.7 |
| **Other** | | |
| Make or grow them myself | 91 | 17.6 |
| From other informal sector producer/retailer | 83 | 16.0 |
| From another country | 51 | 9.8 |
| From home country | 39 | 7.5 |
| N | 518 | |
| Note: multiple response question | | |

A common assertion is that employment creation by migrant entrepreneurs is limited to family members and people from their own countries.[35] This may be true in Delft, a township on the outskirts of Cape Town, but is not replicated across the city as a whole. The migrant entrepreneurs surveyed created a total of 644 jobs including family employment, or 496 jobs excluding family employment (Table 16). Of the 496 non-family jobs, 282 (or 57%) went to South Africans. At the time of the survey, 21% of the migrant entrepreneurs employed their own family members in their business, 18% employed people from their home country and 12% employed migrants from other countries (Table 17). By creating employment for their family members and home country peers, it could be argued that they are actually reducing the unemployment problem in South Africa by reducing pressure on the over-subscribed job market. In terms of gender, male family members working on a full-time basis outnumbered female employees by a factor of one to two and a half and by one to four for those working on a part-time basis (Table 17). Men also outnumbered women in the hiring of migrants from the home country and other countries.

Table 16: Jobs Created by Migrant Entrepreneurs (Non-Family Employment)

|  | South Africans | | Non-South Africans | | Total | |
|---|---|---|---|---|---|---|
|  | No. | % | No. | % | No. | % |
| Full-time | 203 | 40.9 | 166 | 33 | 369 | 74.4 |
| Part-time | 79 | 15.9 | 48 | 10 | 127 | 25.6 |
| Total | 282 | 56.9 | 214 | 43.1 | 496 | 43.1 |

Table 17: Sex of Employees of Migrant Entrepreneurs in Cape Town

| No. of employees | | Family members | | Home country peers | | South Africans | | People from other countries | |
|---|---|---|---|---|---|---|---|---|---|
|  |  | N | % | N | % | N | % | N | % |
| Full time — male | 1 | 49 | 9.5 | 38 | 7.3 | 35 | 6.8 | 27 | 5.2 |
|  | 2 | 9 | 1.7 | 12 | 2.3 | 11 | 2.1 | 5 | 1.0 |
|  | 3 | 1 | 0.2 | 2 | 0.4 | 3 | 0.6 | 1 | 0.2 |
|  | 4 | 2 | 0.4 | 1 | 0.2 | 0 | 0.0 | 0 | 0.0 |
|  | 5 | 1 | 0.2 | 2 | 0.4 | 0 | 0.0 | 0 | 0.0 |
| Full time — female | 1 | 23 | 4.4 | 14 | 2.7 | 73 | 14.1 | 9 | 1.7 |
|  | 2 | 1 | 0.2 | 4 | 0.8 | 23 | 4.4 | 5 | 1.0 |
|  | 3 | 0 | 0.0 | 0 | 0.0 | 6 | 1.2 | 1 | 0.2 |
| Part time — male | 1 | 13 | 2.5 | 6 | 1.2 | 16 | 3.1 | 9 | 1.7 |
|  | 2 | 7 | 1.4 | 3 | 0.6 | 7 | 1.4 | 2 | 0.4 |
|  | 3 | 1 | 0.2 | 1 | 0.2 | 0 | 0.0 | 1 | 0.2 |
|  | 4 | 1 | 0.2 | 1 | 0.2 | 0 | 0.0 | 0 | 0.0 |

| Part time | 1 | 4 | 0.8 | 6 | 1.2 | 34 | 6.6 | 5 | 1.0 |
|---|---|---|---|---|---|---|---|---|---|
| — female | 2 | 1 | 0.2 | 1 | 0.2 | 6 | 1.2 | 0 | 0.0 |
| | 3 | 0 | 0.0 | 0 | 0.0 | 1 | 0.2 | 0 | 0.0 |
| N=518 | | | | | | | | | |

As many as 41% of the entrepreneurs employed South Africans, a rather unexpected finding given the well-documented and widespread negative attitudes of the latter towards migrants and refugees. Unlike with family members and home country peers, there is a general preference for hiring females when employing South Africans. Thus, while 20% of the businesses employ female South Africans on a full-time basis, only 9% employ male South Africans. Similarly, while 8% of the businesses employ female South Africans on a part-time basis, only 4% employ male South Africans on a part-time basis. In other words, not only are migrant entrepreneurs creating jobs for South Africans, they show a distinct and welcome gender bias in that they employ more female than male South Africans. In a labour market that discriminates against women, this contribution to greater gender equity should not be overlooked.

Migrant entrepreneurs are certainly aware of what the employment of South Africans means for them and their families. As one focus group participant noted:

> I make clothes, especially African attires. My business is contributing to the economy. I think it is contributing in reducing the number of people who are unemployed and therefore reducing crime in South Africa. The people who are working for me are able to get money to buy food or help some other people in need and their families.[36]

Another commented at length on the perception that migrants take rather than create jobs and the xenophobia to which this gives rise:

> You see, many people say we take jobs. No, that is not right, we do not take jobs, but we create jobs. I came with my brother from Pakistan and started our small shop. We had R2,000, maybe R3,000. It was not much so we started small. Selling small things like cell-phone chargers, glasses (spectacles), shoe polish, nail polish, just small things. We were selling on the street and displaying on a box. But later we rented a stall from a guy who wanted to go to a bigger shop. So now we had a small stall and we are selling food: drinks, biscuits, chips, fish and other

*things. Now we have three shops. We sell everything and we work hard. Two people we employ are South Africans. We pay fair. But you see sometimes they steal, and so they go. The ones I am working with now are good and two years they are with me, so I do not complain. I help them, they help me. They speak Xhosa and can talk to customers. I know little Xhosa, but we make business. But you see, some people don't like it. They want us to close down. Some want us to go away. The government says we can stay and then some people just think we can just go and leave everything. If we go, we sell. But who is going to run the shops? I don't know.*[37]

Several respondents commented not only on their job creation for South Africans but their skills transfer potential:

*If you don't have experience in the business to speak to people and to manage the business, you can come to us to get experience. Here I employ three people. I pay their salary from the money we make here. They are all South African. They help me operate the business. They know the language and can help me get customers.*[38]

*You can see here that we are nine people; we used to be 11 people. So if a man comes and says he wants to be part of this, why should we refuse him? Five people here are South Africans, two Malawians and two Nigerians. There used to be a Congolese here, but he left. So there are jobs for any race. It doesn't matter where you come from, we are not like some people practising racism. No, we are free, we can chat with the customers, we are all Africans and the spirit of Africa is reigning in this shop.*[39]

*The people here (South Africans) did not know anything about plaiting hair. We have taught them. I don't think this business will endure if all of the Congolese ladies in the industry were told to go back home. This business has contributed a lot to South African women's development.*[40]

Finally, there is the role that migrant entrepreneurs play in making affordable goods and services available to poorer consumers in the city. In this study, we interviewed a furniture repairer who bought and restored broken furniture for sale, a woman who had acquired an old sewing machine and made clothes for sale, and a number of entrepreneurs in the hair-style business, including hairdressers, barbers and vendors of hair products:

*I make South African outfits and this place is mainly for South Africans. So most South Africans benefit from this. I buy my materials for them and tailor for them. I buy my materials in East London.*[41]

*As you see, we don't have real electricity. We are just using our own skills in technology to obtain electricity. This is a battery with a converter and we have electricity. When South Africans see such a thing, they encourage us. They promise us their support and say they will come to our barber shop. We don't have customers other than South Africans themselves. Our own people are just too few.*[42]

Those involved in food vending not only provide an important service, they also contribute to the formal food economy:

*This business is very important to us and the people of South Africa. Early in the morning, the people need food and tea and other things. We make it ready for them as they come here to get something to eat. The products are delivered to us by Coke, Jive and others. And this bread is also brought here by the Wholesome Bread company truck. Every morning they come to deliver here by truck. All these products are local products, manufactured here in South Africa. We don't import outside products.*[43]

## MOBILITY AND CROSS-BORDER LINKAGES

### IMPORT AND EXPORT OF GOODS

Informal traders are able to move goods across boundaries with relative ease and may own businesses in more than one country. Thus, the current study sought to document the international connections maintained by migrant entrepreneurs in Cape Town. These include export and import of goods as well as international business ownership. However, since only 2% of the respondents export goods from South Africa, their participation in international trade is limited. A larger number (19%) import goods into South Africa. Imported items include handcrafts or curios; cosmetics and hair items; new clothes and shoes; DVDs and CDs; fresh, tinned and dried fish; traditional medicine; and textiles. In terms of the origin of imported goods, Zimbabwe is the top source country, followed by the DRC, Nigeria, China, Malawi, Mozambique and Kenya. Zimbabwe dominates as the source country of handicrafts and curios, while the DRC is an important source of cosmetics. Chinese traders were mentioned as a common source for goods from China:

> Like most migrant businesses in Cape Town, we get our supplies from other migrants that import from China, and sometimes we buy from Chinese wholesalers in Cape Town, or Chinese centres in Ottery, and also we get our supplies from Chinese importers. A few times, we go and buy stocks from Johannesburg.[44]

Another question to ask about migrant entrepreneurship in South Africa is whether the entrepreneurs own businesses in other countries with ties to the business they operate in South Africa. However, only 5% of the migrant entrepreneurs who participated in the survey owned businesses outside South Africa (almost exclusively in their countries of origin) that had direct links with their business in Cape Town.

## REMITTANCES

Remittances are known to spur development in the home country of migrants whether they are used for consumption or investment purposes.[45] With respect to migrant entrepreneurs' remitting behaviour, several questions arise. First, to what extent does informal migrant ownership contribute to development and inclusive growth in countries of origin? Second, to what extent does the practice of sending remittances by entrepreneurs encourage or support the growth of informal money transfer channels? Third, do the remitting patterns of the entrepreneurs have an effect on the growth trajectories of their businesses? Finally, are the migrant entrepreneurs themselves recipients of remittances from other countries which could potentially encourage the growth of their businesses?

The frequency of sending remittances is an important measure of the strength of ties that migrants maintain with their country of origin. As many as 60% of the respondents can be categorized as regular remitters, sending remittances to people in their home country at least a few times a year (Figure 7). Only 23% do not send money at all to their home countries. At least half of those who have never sent money have been in South Africa for less than five years and probably lack the resources to remit. Remittances are sent largely to immediate and extended family members (95%). Less than 2% send money to be deposited in a bank account for use on return and less than 1% send remittances to community groups or organizations in their home country.

Figure 7: Frequency of Sending Remittances

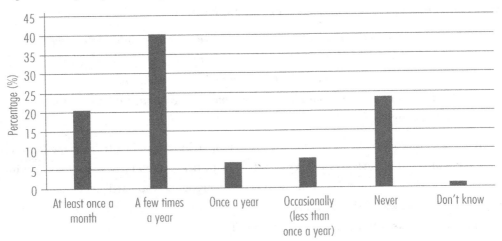

Formal money transfer agencies such as MoneyGram and Western Union (used by 40% of the respondents) were extremely popular when sending money to the home country (Figure 8). Banks were used by a further 20%. Thus, nearly 60% of the entrepreneurs rely on formal transfer channels to send remittances. The widespread utilization of formal channels is a further economic advantage to South Africa since it boosts local financial institutions that benefit from the transfer fees. Informal money transfer channels were used by 17% of the respondents while others preferred to send money with family members, friends or co-workers (14%) or took it themselves (6%). There is a popular perception that migrants clandestinely channel resources from South Africa. On the contrary, although entrepreneurs are denied access to credit from financial institutions, these findings demonstrate that they still support local banks and money transfer companies when remitting.

The migrant entrepreneurs remit an average of ZAR9,159 per annum. This is a significant sum given that most of the entrepreneurs make an average annual profit of about ZAR48,000 per annum. The average amount remitted annually represents more than two months of net earnings, which might have implications for the growth of the business. However, only 15% of the respondents said that sending remittances had a negative impact on their business. More (21%) actually see sending remittances as positive for the business, which could be because of the peace of mind of knowing that their family in the home country is taken care of. This conclusion is supported by the use to which the remittances are put (Table 18), including buying food (60%), meeting other household expenses (49%), paying education fees (44%), buying clothes (40%) and paying medical bills (35%). Only a small proportion (less than 10%) use the money for investment purposes such as building or renovating dwellings, buying property, purchasing agricultural inputs or equipment (6%) or for starting or running a business.

Figure 8: Money Transfer Channels Used by Migrant Entrepreneurs

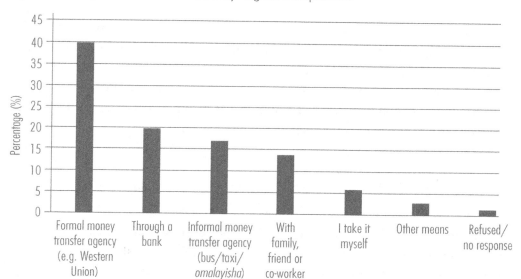

Table 18: Reasons for Remitting to Home Country

|  | No. | % of total |
|---|---|---|
| Buy food | 311 | 60.2 |
| Meet day-to-day household expenses (except food) | 252 | 48.7 |
| Pay educational/school fees | 228 | 44.1 |
| Buy clothes | 204 | 39.5 |
| Pay medical expenses | 181 | 35.0 |
| For special events e.g. wedding and funeral expenses | 99 | 19.1 |
| Pay transportation costs | 40 | 7.7 |
| Build, maintain or renovate their dwelling | 40 | 7.7 |
| Buy property | 32 | 6.2 |
| For agricultural inputs/ equipment | 30 | 5.8 |

| | | |
|---|---|---|
| For savings investment | 23 | 4.4 |
| Purchase livestock | 14 | 2.7 |
| Start or run a business | 6 | 1.2 |
| Other reasons | 6 | 1.2 |
| Note: multiple response question | | |

Only 7% of the respondents indicated that they received remittances from other countries, including from their family in the home country and family members living in other countries. The amounts received are not substantial, averaging around ZAR13,071 per annum. Remittances received from other countries are largely invested in business growth. Of the 30 respondents who received remittances from other countries, 80% noted that receiving remittances had positive implications for their business.

## BUSINESS CHALLENGES

The research sought to examine the problems and challenges migrant entrepreneurs face in running a successful business operation in Cape Town. Nineteen potential challenges were presented to the respondents who were asked to indicate whether they experienced the problems often, sometimes or never. For purposes of analysis, the potential challenges were grouped into economic, social, security and other categories (Table 19). It becomes immediately clear that the main challenges faced by the migrant entrepreneurs, like business owners everywhere, are economic. Competition is fierce in the informal economy and half of the respondents said they had too many competitors (with 80% often/sometimes experiencing this problem). Related economic challenges were too few customers (94%) and insufficient sales (92%). Less important, but by no means insignificant, were suppliers charging too much (64%), a lack of credit (54%) and customers not paying their debts (50%).

In the Cape Town context, recent research has focused on the expansion of supermarkets throughout the city.[46] A key unanswered question is whether supermarkets are undermining the informal economy. Only 14% of the entrepreneurs felt they were often affected by competition from supermarkets, although the number rose to 45% for those often and sometimes affected.

Table 19: Business Challenges and Problems

|  | Often (%) | Sometimes (%) | Never (%) |
|---|---|---|---|
| **Economic challenges** | | | |
| Too many competitors around here | 49.4 | 31.1 | 19.5 |
| Lack of access to credit | 34.1 | 19.9 | 46.0 |
| Insufficient sales | 24.4 | 67.4 | 8.2 |
| Too few customers | 22.4 | 72.1 | 5.5 |
| Suppliers charge too much | 16.8 | 48.9 | 34.3 |
| Competition from supermarkets/large stores | 14.4 | 31.1 | 54.5 |
| Customers don't pay their debts | 10.5 | 40.0 | 49.4 |
| **Social challenges** | | | |
| Prejudice against my nationality | 13.7 | 35.4 | 51.0 |
| Verbal insults against my business | 11.2 | 22.9 | 65.9 |
| Conflict with other entrepreneurs | 6.8 | 32.8 | 60.4 |
| Prejudice against my gender | 1.0 | 5.5 | 93.5 |
| **Security challenges** | | | |
| Crime/theft | 27.8 | 45.4 | 26.8 |
| Confiscation of goods | 7.7 | 28.1 | 64.2 |
| Physical attacks/assaults by South Africans | 7.1 | 28.9 | 64 |
| Harassment/demands for bribes by police | 5.5 | 20.3 | 74.2 |
| Arrest/detention of yourself/employees | 5.2 | 12.4 | 82.5 |
| Physical attacks/assaults by police | 2.7 | 12.3 | 84.9 |
| **Other** | | | |
| Storage problems | 13.2 | 23.3 | 63.4 |
| Lack of relevant business training | 5.5 | 18.9 | 75.6 |

The in-depth interviews and focus groups provided additional insights into the economic challenges facing the entrepreneurs. For example, for those whose business is tied to tourism, the challenges are greater in the off-season:

> *Whenever it is time for tourism, the season I mean, people, a lot of people, come to Cape Town and buy. But when winter comes, we face a lot of problems. There are few or no customers to come and buy because it's cold and they don't come.*[47]

41

One of the interview respondents attributed the problem of low sales to the global economic crisis, which has restricted most people from spending beyond their basic needs:

> *There are few customers who are buying as they used to before. Because in the past years the customers were coming, they were buying. But I think because of the global financial crisis, they are not buying much anymore. They are budgeting their money and not spending a lot. We need customers to buy our goods. Our business depends on customers who come to buy. So my problems have to do with low sales. It's really affecting most people here. You can go for days without selling anything and you are expected to pay rent and other costs.*[48]

Intense competition, particularly in the hair services sector, was mentioned by several migrant entrepreneurs who were struggling to make a profit:

> *I plait hair. This business used to be good before, but currently it seems it is not moving at all because there are too many people offering the same service. The other issue is that we don't support each other. You can find that maybe we have the same marketplace and have agreed the price, but one just decides to reduce the price to attract more clients to her. Currently the money is not enough. We just come and sit, we get cold and then we leave. We should be able to get R2,000 per week but these days you can only get R150 or R200. This is just a lot of suffering when you have to pay the owner of the place. We are seeing that this is the end of the industry now. We have messed it up ourselves. We have brought ourselves down by overcharging and over-competing.*[49]

> *Before I was able to get R1,000 in a week. But currently it's very difficult just to get R200 in a week. That means there's no more money in circulation and there are not enough women coming for plaiting hair like before. Currently, it's very difficult just to pay for this place. We normally pay for it by the 5th but now we can even go up to the 10th. Maybe I should go back to school because the hair business is not successful anymore.*[50]

As noted earlier, very few migrant and refugee entrepreneurs are able to get bank loans for their businesses. Lack of access to credit was identified as a problem by 54% of the respondents. Participants in focus group discussions and in-depth interviews indicated that South African banks have a very negative attitude towards non-South African entrepreneurs:

*The banks do not see us as business people. They see us as foreigners first, so you may not even get the chance to say I am a business person, so please can I have money. They just say do you have ID and if you say no, then they will tell you that they cannot help. So, they do not see us as business people. We are migrants, we are foreigners and that's that.*[51]

*I think there is some criteria they (banks) use in order to give credit. I think we are not fitting the criteria, being foreigners. Maybe others think that if they give us the money they won't know where to find us. The first priority when you are getting a credit or a loan from a bank, you must be a South African or have an ID. We are not South Africans, we are refugees, we fled our country from a civil war. Being a refugee, you get asylum from the government [but] as you go to bank as a refugee automatically you are not qualified to have a loan.*[52]

*Capital is the biggest problem. Where do you get capital? I tried before, you know, to get money from a bank, but I did not succeed. I have no green book, that is what they told me. And I can also just leave without paying back the loan. That is what they said. So, I think it is difficult to get money to start a business if you are a foreigner.*[53]

Migrant entrepreneurs also face significant security challenges. South Africa has an extremely high crime rate but there is also evidence that migrants are disproportionately affected by violence.[54] Some of this can be attributed to business competition or what has been labelled "violent entrepreneurship" where attacks are orchestrated by South African competitors.[55] As one Somali entrepreneur observed:

*The main problem that we are facing is competition, which is creating hatred between local business owners and Somali business owners, whereby locals are trying to mobilize the community around them to take advantage of that process.*[56]

However, theft and looting of migrants businesses by ordinary citizens, including children, is also common. As many as 28% of the entrepreneurs said they were often victims of theft and crime and another 45% said this was sometimes the case. This means that three-quarters of the respondents saw crime and theft as a significant challenge to their operations. Physical attacks and assault by South Africans were of concern to 36% of the respondents. Some felt that they are systematically targeted by criminals who know that the police will not help:

> *They do not steal from us just because we are foreigners. They are just thieves and they steal everywhere. But maybe they know that foreigners will not be helped by police and they steal.*[57]

Many respondents claimed that, even when crimes are reported, the police do not take any steps to apprehend the criminals:

> *Actually their reaction is very low. Because I was robbed twice, and the second time it was captured on the CCTV cameras, they took the footage of the CCTV cameras, and they have never responded to us. Never, not even came back to us and ask about and give us feedback of the investigation. Even our investigation officer, it was our first and the last time that we have seen him, the day of robbery. So that means they are not even considering you as part of the community.*[58]

The attitudes and actions of police were also a significant concern for entrepreneurs. A quarter said that demands for bribes by the police were a challenge. Even more (36%) said the confiscation of goods by the police was a problem. Fewer, but certainly not insignificant, numbers said that police arrests were a challenge with which they had to deal (15%). The same number cited physical assaults by the police as a significant problem.

Nearly 50% of the entrepreneurs mentioned discrimination against people of their nationality as a problem and a third said that they had to endure verbal assaults from South Africans. Some, for example reported on the hostility as follows:

> *You are aware that the people here don't really like us around. Yet we came here just to look for survival. The locals don't like us because they think we have come to get their jobs. It's too hard and it has become like a war. We are not enjoying peace at all. They don't really know this job but they are just jealous of seeing us do this job. So instead of coming to learn how we are doing it, they come and rob us.*[59]

> *Some people are rude, some are kind, and some don't care about you. Even after you cut their hair some people will just start insulting you "Hey you foreigner!" There are some citizens who would just want to give you that kind of hassle. The reason we don't give up is because we don't want to be in the street. We make sure we put food on the table for the kids, pay the children's school fees and pay our rent.*[60]

*I lost goods in the past. We really fear that. It was the day the people were marching here in town and they started rioting and vandalizing. We reported the matter to the police but nothing has been done. Another day they came here with knives. They could not do anything physically but just insulted people here: "Hey, you foreigners, makwerekwere."[61]*

A number of studies have demonstrated the impact of xenophobia on the livelihoods of migrants and refugees in South Africa.[62] An emerging literature has also started to examine the specific impact of xenophobia on the business enterprises of immigrants.[63] Asked whether their businesses had been affected by xenophobia, 18% said they had been affected "a great deal" and 27% "to some extent". Thus, nearly half of the respondents in total (45%) have had their business operations affected by xenophobia. Where a migrant comes from appears to influence how susceptible their business operations are to xenophobia (Table 20). For example, 68% of Cameroonians, 66% of Somalis, 50% of Congolese, 49% of Ethiopians, 45% of Kenyans and 41% of Nigerians said their business was affected by xenophobia. Notably, most of the entrepreneurs from three of these countries (the DRC, Somalia and Ethiopia) are refugees. By contrast, only 30% of Zimbabweans said their business was affected by xenophobia, which might be due to the fact that Zimbabweans are regarded more positively by South Africans. However, this conclusion is belied by other evidence.[64] Alternatively, it could be that Somalis and Ethiopians, in particular, are more willing to run their businesses in the townships despite these areas being hotbeds of xenophobia.

Table 20: Extent to which Xenophobia Affects Business Operations by Home Country

|  | A great deal/to some extent (%) | Not very much/not at all (%) |
|---|---|---|
| **SADC** | | |
| DRC | 50.0 | 50.0 |
| Malawi | 43.6 | 56.4 |
| Zimbabwe | 30.5 | 69.5 |
| **Other Africa** | | |
| Cameroon | 68.2 | 31.8 |
| Somalia | 64.3 | 35.7 |
| Ethiopia | 48.6 | 51.4 |
| Nigeria | 41.7 | 58.3 |
| Kenya | 45.5 | 54.5 |

| | | |
|---|---|---|
| Ghana | 41.2 | 58.8 |
| Congo Brazzaville | 38.5 | 61.5 |
| Uganda | 33.3 | 66.7 |
| *Note: only countries with 10 or more respondents included* | | |

Certainly, xenophobia has become a strong consideration in the choice of business sites by the migrant entrepreneurs. Some avoid locating their businesses in townships altogether. This means that they prefer running their businesses in the city centre where the levels of xenophobia are perceived to be lower, with the downside that they experience intense competition from other traders:

> *You see, this thing about xenophobia is just bad. It is very bad. Some people in South Africa are not friendly. They think all foreigners should go. But if the government allows us to stay, then why are the people harassing us? I do not understand it. The government should just tell us if they want us to stay or go. I have a lot of friends that are affected by xenophobia. They have shops and stalls in the townships and that is where xenophobia is bad. The people come and take your goods and your stock is taken just like that. You will take months to recover and have to borrow from other people to restock. Thieves also take advantage of xenophobia and they steal and nothing is done. So, most people are not comfortable going to the townships, and that is why there are a lot of us here in the CBD. But now that affects our profits and we have to share the few customers and get very little.[65]*

## CONCLUSION

This report began with the recent military-style assault on informal traders, both migrant and South African, at the Cape Town railway station. While this whole operation seemed like massive overkill and certainly mystified the traders themselves (apart from costing them a day's business and the loss of their hard-earned goods), it is not the first time that the power of the central and local state has been directed at the city's informal economy. Indeed, as this report demonstrates, a significant number of migrant and refugee entrepreneurs throughout the city have been victims of police misconduct in the form of physical and verbal assault, arbitrary arrests and confiscation of goods without cause. Migrant entrepreneurs trying to tap the township and informal settlement markets take their lives into their hands because, they claim, they receive no police protection and the police do not arrest those who attack them. The proportion of migrant entrepreneurs (even those who do not go near the townships and informal settlements) who have been victims of crimes is extraordinarily high. Clearly, the agents of law and order on the ground are not providing even the most basic protections and, in some cases, are participants in creating an unsafe environment for business (by commission and omission).[66]

One of the reasons for the aversion, uncertainty and stereotyping of migrant entrepreneurs on the streets and in the corridors of municipal power may be the relatively recent penetration of Cape Town's informal economy by migrants and refugees. Very few of the respondents in this study came to South Africa before 2000 and the vast majority established their businesses in the city after 2005. If this is the case, then a serious effort needs to be made to educate the public, the police and officials about what migrant entrepreneurs offer the city. All too often, it is the supposed negative impacts that gain all the media attention – putting South Africans out of business, engaging in nefarious and underhand business practices, purveying illegal goods and firing back when they are attacked by mobs of looters. When service delivery protests against the state turn into violent attacks on migrant businesses, as they did in 2013, there is clearly something badly amiss in the public perception of the role and value of migrant entrepreneurship.[67]

This report is the most comprehensive study yet of the contribution of migrant and refugee entrepreneurs to Cape Town's local economy. The survey of over 500 entrepreneurs engaged in trade, services and manufacturing in different areas of the city dispels some of the more prevalent myths that often attach to the activities of migrants. First, the vast majority are not "illegal foreigners" in the provocative language of the Immigration Act, but have a legal right to be in South Africa and to run a business. Second, the majority are not "survivalists", forced into the informal economy out of poverty and desperation. Instead, they are highly motivated individuals who enter the informal economy to earn revenue to support themselves, their families, and their relatives in their home country (through remittances) and because they have a strong entrepreneurial motivation. Also, they view themselves as performing a broader social and economic function; that is, contributing to the development of South Africa.

Third, contrary to the claims of South African competitors, the vast majority are not successful because they are engaged in shadowy and illicit business practices. Even perfectly legitimate practices, such as group bulk buying from suppliers, are not as widespread as is often claimed. What emerges from the survey is that while migrant and refugee entrepreneurs undoubtedly have strong social networks at the personal level, their businesses are highly individualistic in terms of organization, ownership and activity in a highly competitive business environment.

Who, then, benefits from their presence in Cape Town? First, city coffers benefit in terms of payments by those occupying business premises for which the City charges rents. This amounted to a third of the entrepreneurs in total. South African property owners also benefit by renting stands to migrants and refugees. Again, about a third of the entrepreneurs pay rentals to South Africans. Two-thirds of the entrepreneurs, despite being in the informal economy, thus pay rent to the municipality or South African property owners. In total, this means a total of ZAR9.7 million per year, just from this sample of respondents. The total figure from all entrepreneurs would be very much higher.

The third group of beneficiaries are those from whom the entrepreneurs purchase their goods and supplies. These include wholesalers, small shops and retailers, supermarkets, factories and the Epping fresh produce market. Wholesalers benefit the most with two-thirds of the entrepreneurs sourcing goods from their outlets. Only a few entrepreneurs source goods from another country or their home country, although some travel to other South African cities such as Johannesburg to purchase goods for resale in Cape Town. There is a tendency – inherent in descriptions of the informal economy as the "second economy" – to view formal and informal business as separate entities. This is an artificial division in the Cape Town context. Informal businesses constantly interact with formal suppliers, to the obvious financial benefit of the latter.

The fourth group of beneficiaries are the unemployed and job-seekers. Contrary to popular perceptions that entrepreneurs only hire their own, this study revealed that informal businesses also generate employment for South Africans. The migrant entrepreneurs interviewed for this study employed a total of 644 people (or 1.1 jobs per business). Of these, 496 were non-family and 282 (or 57%) were South Africans. As many as 41% of the entrepreneurs employed South Africans. By creating employment of any kind, they are contributing to the alleviation of the unemployment problem in South Africa. However, noting their specific employment of South Africans, it becomes more difficult to sustain the common xenophobic argument that all migrants do is "steal" jobs from South Africans.

As noted at the outset of this report, the Mayor of Cape Town made extremely positive and encouraging remarks about the importance of the informal economy to the City at the 2013 Summit on Informal Traders. To prove that this was not simply rhetoric, the City took a very critical public stance on the moribund draft Licensing of Businesses Bill tabled by the Minister of Trade and Industry, which threatened to overwhelm small businesses and the municipality with red tape and would give the police free reign to drive informal businesses to the wall. What was not clear from De Lille's supportive remarks is whether she was referring to all informal vendors or only those with South African citizenship. If she was typical of the municipal authorities in many South African cities, as well as politicians like the Minister of Small Business Development, Lindiwe Zulu, her support would have been largely confined to South Africans.[68] At the same time, De Lille also loudly condemned the nationwide xenophobic violence in early 2015. In a strong public statement – "City Stands United Against Xenophobia" – she proclaimed that "some among us have turned against the brothers and sisters from the very nations who assisted us in our struggle against apartheid. We cannot allow this to continue. We cannot let this be done, in the name of our country, South Africa."[69]

The challenge facing the Mayor is to bring these two streams together in her own mind, in the ranks of city officials, and among ordinary Capetonians. In other words, xenophobia needs to be purged from the informal economy and those who claim to police and regulate it. There is enough evidence in this report to suggest both that xenophobia is a significant, and unnecessary, business challenge for migrant and refugee entrepreneurs who are often vilified and not sufficiently protected to go about their business as usual. Xenophobia and associated negative attitudes and regulations also pose significant business challenges to a group of extremely hard-working entrepreneurs whose efforts would be praised in most other contexts. Instead of having them give up their "secrets" of success to their competitors, as the Minister of Small Business Development recently demanded, it would make much more sense to support their efforts through bank loans, micro-credit schemes and business skills development, if only to create economic benefit and additional jobs for all.[70] Or as one of the focus group participants presciently observed:

> South Africa allowed us to live here so we have to do something to help ourselves and also help the people that provide us with the place to live. I am happy about that... We are grateful to South Africa for allowing us to stay here. So we appreciate that. We are here to do our bit. We will work and try as much as we

*can to operate our businesses and help each other. But we need the government to protect us and make conditions better for us to survive. We are not here to steal jobs. We are here to create jobs and help ourselves. South African people must not see us as enemies. We are not enemies. We are just people trying to make a living. We can work together, and they can learn from us. Like my South African sister that works for me. Now she is able to do plaiting and a lot of hair styles that she learned from me. We can do that with a lot of other people if they do not scare us, or steal and threaten us.*[71]

# ENDNOTES

1    City of Cape Town, "Speech by the Executive Mayor of Cape Town, Alderman Patricia De Lille on the Occasion of a Summit for Informal Traders Hosted by the City, 20 March 2013" Media Release No. 1260/ 2013.

2    Y. Kamaldien, "Foreigners Held in Cape Fiela Swoop" *IOL News* 21 June 2015.

3    Patricia Kawe, 60, of Khayelitsha, quoted in B. Chiguvare, "Army Closes Down Cape Town Station" *GroundUp* 22 June 2015.

4    Noluvuyo Faye, informal trader, 32, Gugulethu, quoted in R. Pather, "Operation Fiela in the Cape Town CBD" *The Daily Vox* 23 June 2015.

5    Mwanyange Ubao Mohamed, 37, informal trader, Salt River, from Tanzania, quoted in Pather "Operation Fiela."

6    Fatima Nyondo, 26, hairdresser, Lansdowne, from Malawi, quoted in Pather, "Operation Fiela."

7    Philemon Nji Kum, 33, student at Cape Peninsula University of Technology and clothing trader, from Cameroon, quoted in Chiguvare, "Army Closes Down Cape Town Station."

8    V. Gastrow, "Business Robbery, the Foreign Trader and the Small Shop" *SA Quarterly* 43(2013): 5-16.

9    IRIN News, "Somalia-South Africa: Foreign Competitors Not Welcome" 17 October 2008.

10   https://www.facebook.com/SomaliSouthAfrica

11   Gastrow, "Business Robbery" p. 8.

12   Ibid., p. 11.

13   V. Kalitanyi, "Evaluation of Employment Creation by African Immigrant Entrepreneurs for Unemployed South Africans in Cape Town" M.Comm. Thesis, University of the Western Cape, 2007; V. Kalitanyi and K. Visser, "African Immigrants in South Africa: Job Takers or Job Creators?" *South African Journal of Economic and Management Sciences*, 13(2010): 376-90; A. Charman and L. Piper, "Xenophobia, Criminality and Violent Entrepreneurship: Violence against Somali Shopkeepers in Delft South, Cape Town, South Africa" *South African Review of Sociology* 43(2012): 81-105; A.

Charman, L. Petersen and L. Piper, "From Local Survivalism to Foreign Entrepreneurship: The Transformation of the Spaza Sector in Delft, Cape Town" *Transformation: Critical Perspectives on Southern Africa* 78(2012): 47–73; R. Tengeh, "A Business Framework for the Effective Start-up and Operation of African Immigrant-Owned Businesses in the Cape Town Metropolitan Area, South Africa" PhD Thesis, Cape Peninsula University of Technology, 2012; V. Gastrow and R. Amit, "Somalinomics: A Case Study on the Economic Dimensions of Somali Informal Trade in the Western Cape" ACMS Report, University of the Witwatersrand, 2013; B. Mwasinga, "Assessing the Implications of Local Governance on Street Trading: A Case of Cape Town's Inner City" Masters in City and Regional Planning Thesis, University of Cape Town, 2013; C. Lapah and R. Tengeh, "The Migratory Trajectories of the Post-1994 Generation of African Immigrants to South Africa: An Empirical Study of Street Vendors in the Cape Town Metropolitan Area" *Mediterranean Journal of Social Sciences* 4(2013): 181-95; T. Washinyira, "Cape Town: Immigrants Accuse Cops of Abuse as Their Businesses are Destroyed" *Daily Maverick* 27 June 2013; F. Basardien, H. Parker, M. Bayat, C. Friedrich and A. Sulaiman, "Entrepreneurial Orientation of Spaza Shop Entrepreneurs: Evidence from a Study of South African and Somali-owned Spaza Shop Entrepreneurs in Khayelitsha" *Singaporean Journal of Business Economics and Management Studies* 2(2014): 45-61; A. Bukasa, "Securing Sustainable Livelihoods: A Critical Assessment of the City of Cape Town's Approach to Inner City Street Trading" MA Thesis, University of Cape Town, 2014; R. Khosa, "An Analysis of Challenges in Running Micro-Enterprises: A Case of African Foreign Entrepreneurs in Cape Town, Western Cape" M.Tech. Thesis, Cape Peninsula University of Technology, Cape Town, 2014; R. Khosa and V. Kalitanyi, "Challenges in Operating Micro-Enterprises by African Foreign Entrepreneurs in Cape Town, South Africa" *Mediterranean Journal of Social Sciences* 5(2014): 205-215; Gastrow, "Business Robbery", Charman and Piper, "Xenophobia, Criminality and Violent Entrepreneurship."

14  J. Crush and D. Tevera, eds., *Zimbabwe's Exodus: Crisis, Migration, Survival* (Ottawa and Cape Town: IDRC and SAMP, 2010); J. Crush, A. Chikanda and G. Tawodzera, *The Third Wave: Mixed Migration from Zimbabwe to South Africa*, SAMP Migration Policy Series No. 59, Cape Town, 2012.

15  N. Kleist, "Nomads, Sailors and Refugees: A Century of Somali Migration" Sussex Migration Working Paper No. 23, Sussex University, 2004; Z. Jinnah, "Rational Routes? Understanding Somali Migration to South Africa" In M. van der Velde, ed., *Mobility and Migration Choices: Thresholds to Crossing Borders* (Surrey: Ashgate, 2015), pp. 43-54.

16  A. Hammerstad, "Linking South Africa's Immigration Policy and Zimbabwe Diplomacy" Policy Briefing 42, South African Institute of International Affairs, Johannesburg, 2011.

17  A. Betts, "From Persecution to Deprivation: How Refugee Norms Adapt at Implementation" In A. Betts and P. Orchard, eds., *Implementation and World Politics: How International Norms Change Practice* (Oxford: Oxford University Press, 2014), pp. 29-49.

18  Charman and Piper, "Xenophobia, Criminality and Violent Entrepreneurship"; J. Crush, S. Ramachandran and W. Pendleton, *Soft Targets: Xenophobia, Public Violence and Changing Attitudes to Migrants in South Africa After May 2008*, SAMP Migration Policy Series No. 64, Cape Town, 2013;

J. Crush and S. Ramachandran, *Migrant Entrepreneurship and Collective Violence in South Africa*, SAMP Migration Policy Series No. 67, Cape Town, 2014.

19   Z. Jinnah, "Making Home in a Hostile Land: Understanding Somali Identity, Integration, Livelihood and Risks in Johannesburg" *Journal of Sociology and Social Anthropology* 1 (2010): 91-9; V. Gastrow and R. Amit, "Somalinomics: A Case Study on the Economic Dimensions of Somali Informal Trade in the Western Cape" ACMS Report, University of the Witwatersrand, 2013.

20   V. Vijaya, and T. Kamalanabhan, "A Scale to Assess Entrepreneurial Motivation" *Journal of Entrepreneurship* 7(1998): 183-198; Y. Robichaud, E. McGraw and A. Roger, "Toward the Development of a Measuring Instrument for Entrepreneurial Motivation" *Journal of Development Entrepreneurship*, 6(2001): 189-201; S. Shane, E. A. Locke and C. Collins, "Entrepreneurial Motivation" *Human Resource Management Review* 13(2003): 257-79; B. Mitchell, "Motives of Entrepreneurs: A Case Study of South Africa" *Journal of Entrepreneurship* 13(2004): 167-183; O. Fatoki and T. Patswawairi, "The Motivations and Obstacles to Immigrant Entrepreneurship" *Journal of Social Science* 32(2012): 133-42; R. Khosa and V. Kalitanyi, "Migration Reasons, Traits and Entrepreneurial Motivation of African Immigrant Entrepreneurs" *Journal of Enterprising Communities: People and Places in the Global Economy* 9(2015):132-155.

21   Interview with Somali entrepreneur, Bellville, October 2014.

22   Interview with Zimbabwean entrepreneur, Cape Town CBD.

23   Interview with DRC entrepreneur, Bellville.

24   Focus group participant, Cape Town CBD, 21 June 2014.

25   Crush et al., *Soft Targets*; Charman and Piper, "Xenophobia, Criminality and Violent Entrepreneurship."

26   Kalitanyi and Visser, "African Immigrants in South Africa"; N. Radipere, "An Analysis of Local and Immigrant Entrepreneurship in the South African Small Enterprise Sector (Gauteng Province)" PhD Thesis, UNISA, 2012; Tengeh, "Business Framework for Effective Start-up."

27   Interview with female tailor, Philippi.

28   Interview with Nigerian barber-shop owner, Philippi.

29   Interview with Zimbabwean entrepreneur, Cape Town CBD.

30   Interview with Zimbabwean entrepreneur, Cape Town CBD.

31   O. Fatoki, "An Investigation into the Financial Bootstrapping Methods Used by Immigrant Entrepreneurs in South Africa" *Journal of Economics* 4(2013): 89-96; A. Ikuomola and J. Zaaiman, "We Have Come to Stay and We Shall Find All Means to Live and Work in This Country: Nigerian Migrants and Life Challenges in South Africa" *Issues in Ethnology and Anthropology* 9(2014): 371-88.

32   Gastrow and Amit, "Somalinomics".

33   Interview with wholesale manager, Cape Town, 27 June 2014.

34   Kalitanyi, "Evaluation of Employment Creation"; Charman, Petersen and Piper, "From Local Survivalism to Foreign Entrepreneurship."

35  Ibid.; R. Liedeman, "Understanding the Internal Dynamics and Organisation of Spaza Shop Operators" Master's Thesis, University of the Western Cape, 2013.

36  Focus group participant, Cape Town CBD, 21 June 2014.

37  Focus group participant, Cape Town CBD, 21 June 2014.

38  Interview with Somali entrepreneur, Cape Town.

39  Interview with Nigerian barber-shop owner, Philippi.

40  Interview with Congolese entrepreneur, Bellville.

41  Interview with female tailor, Philippi.

42  Interview with Congolese barber, Bellville.

43  Interview with Somali entrepreneur, Cape Town.

44  Interview with Cameroonian entrepreneur, Bellville, October 2014.

45  R. Adams, "Remittances, Poverty, and Investment in Guatemala" In Ç. Özden and M. Schiff (Eds.), *International Migration, Remittances, and the Brain Drain* (Washington D.C. and Basingstoke: World Bank and Palgrave Macmillan, 2006), pp. 53-80; R. Adams and J. Page, "Do International Migration and Remittances Reduce Poverty in Developing Countries?" *World Development* 33(2005): 1645-69; D. Kapur, "Remittances: The New Development Mantra?" In S. Maimbo and D. Ratha, eds., *Remittances: Development Impact and Future Prospects* (Washington DC: World Bank, 2005), pp. 331-60.

46  J. Crush and B. Frayne, "Supermarket Expansion and the Informal Food Economy in Southern African Cities: Implications for Urban Food Security" *Journal of Southern African Studies* 37(2011): 781-807; J. Battersby and S. Peyton, "The Geography of Supermarkets in Cape Town: Supermarket Expansion and Food Access" *Urban Forum* 25(2014): 153-64; S. Peyton, W. Moseley and J. Battersby, "Implications of Supermarket Expansion on Urban Food Security in Cape Town, South Africa" *African Geographical Review* 34(2015): 36-54.

47  Interview with Zimbabwean trader, Cape Town CBD, October 2014.

48  Interview with Zimbabwean trader, Cape Town CBD, October 2014.

49  Interview with Congolese hairdresser, Bellville.

50  Interview with Congolese hairdresser, Bellville.

51  Focus group participant, Cape Town CBD, 21 June 2014.

52  Interview with Somali entrepreneur, Bellville, October 2014.

53  Focus group participant, Cape Town CBD, 21 June 2014.

54  Gastrow, "Business Robbery"; Crush and Ramachandran, "Migrant Entrepreneurship and Collective Violence in South Africa."

55  Charman and Piper, "Xenophobia, Criminality and Violent Entrepreneurship."

56   Interview with Somali entrepreneur, Philippi, October 2014.

57   Interview with Pakistani entrepreneur, Bellville, October 2014.

58   Interview with Somali entrepreneur, Bellville, October 2014.

59   Interview with Cameroonian entrepreneur, Philippi.

60   Interview with barber, Philippi.

61   Interview with Zimbabwean entrepreneur, Cape Town.

62   C. Abdi, "Moving Beyond Xenophobia: Structural Violence, Conflict and Encounters with the 'Other' Africans" *Development Southern Africa* 28(2011): 691-704; J. Crush, and S. Ramachandran, "Xenophobia, International Migration and Development" *Journal of Human Development and Capabilities* 11(2010): 209-228.

63   J. Crush, A. Chikanda, and C. Skinner, eds., *Mean Streets: Migration, Xenophobia and Informality in South Africa* (Cape Town: SAMP, IDRC and ACC, 2015).

64   J. Crush and G. Tawodzera, "Medical Xenophobia and Zimbabwean Migrant Access to Health Services in South Africa" *Journal of Ethnic and Migration Studies* 40(2014): 655-70.

65   Focus group participant, Cape Town CBD, 21 June 2014.

66   J. Crush and S. Ramachandran, "Doing Business with Xenophobia" In Crush, Chikanda and Skinner, *Mean Streets.*

67   ECNA, "Cape Town Braces for Service Delivery Protest" 29 November 2013.

68   L. Steyn, "Mind Your Own Business, Minister" *Mail & Guardian* 30 January 2015.

69   https://www.capetown.gov.za/en/mayor/Documents/DeLille_speeches/Statement_City_united_against_xenophobia.pdf.

70   K. Magubane, "Reveal Trade Secrets, Minister Tells Foreigners" *Business Day* 25 January 2015.

71   Focus group participant, Cape Town CBD, 21 June 2014.

# MIGRATION POLICY SERIES

1   *Covert Operations: Clandestine Migration, Temporary Work and Immigration Policy in South Africa* (1997) ISBN 1-874864-51-9

2   *Riding the Tiger: Lesotho Miners and Permanent Residence in South Africa* (1997) ISBN 1-874864-52-7

3   *International Migration, Immigrant Entrepreneurs and South Africa's Small Enterprise Economy* (1997) ISBN 1-874864-62-4

4   *Silenced by Nation Building: African Immigrants and Language Policy in the New South Africa* (1998) ISBN 1-874864-64-0

5   *Left Out in the Cold? Housing and Immigration in the New South Africa* (1998) ISBN 1-874864-68-3

6   *Trading Places: Cross-Border Traders and the South African Informal Sector* (1998) ISBN 1-874864-71-3

7   *Challenging Xenophobia: Myth and Realities about Cross-Border Migration in Southern Africa* (1998) ISBN 1-874864-70-5

8   *Sons of Mozambique: Mozambican Miners and Post-Apartheid South Africa* (1998) ISBN 1-874864-78-0

9   *Women on the Move: Gender and Cross-Border Migration to South Africa* (1998) ISBN 1-874864-82-9.

10  *Namibians on South Africa: Attitudes Towards Cross-Border Migration and Immigration Policy* (1998) ISBN 1-874864-84-5.

11  *Building Skills: Cross-Border Migrants and the South African Construction Industry* (1999) ISBN 1-874864-84-5

12  *Immigration & Education: International Students at South African Universities and Technikons* (1999) ISBN 1-874864-89-6

13  *The Lives and Times of African Immigrants in Post-Apartheid South Africa* (1999) ISBN 1-874864-91-8

14  *Still Waiting for the Barbarians: South African Attitudes to Immigrants and Immigration* (1999) ISBN 1-874864-91-8

15  *Undermining Labour: Migrancy and Sub-Contracting in the South African Gold Mining Industry* (1999) ISBN 1-874864-91-8

16  *Borderline Farming: Foreign Migrants in South African Commercial Agriculture* (2000) ISBN 1-874864-97-7

17  *Writing Xenophobia: Immigration and the Press in Post-Apartheid South Africa* (2000) ISBN 1-919798-01-3

18  *Losing Our Minds: Skills Migration and the South African Brain Drain* (2000) ISBN 1-919798-03-x

19  *Botswana: Migration Perspectives and Prospects* (2000) ISBN 1-919798-04-8

20  *The Brain Gain: Skilled Migrants and Immigration Policy in Post-Apartheid South Africa* (2000) ISBN 1-919798-14-5

21  *Cross-Border Raiding and Community Conflict in the Lesotho-South African Border Zone* (2001) ISBN 1-919798-16-1

22  *Immigration, Xenophobia and Human Rights in South Africa* (2001) ISBN 1-919798-30-7

23  *Gender and the Brain Drain from South Africa* (2001) ISBN 1-919798-35-8

24  *Spaces of Vulnerability: Migration and HIV/AIDS in South Africa* (2002) ISBN 1-919798-38-2

25  *Zimbabweans Who Move: Perspectives on International Migration in Zimbabwe* (2002) ISBN 1-919798-40-4

26    *The Border Within: The Future of the Lesotho-South African International Boundary* (2002) ISBN 1-919798-41-2

27    *Mobile Namibia: Migration Trends and Attitudes* (2002) ISBN 1-919798-44-7

28    *Changing Attitudes to Immigration and Refugee Policy in Botswana* (2003) ISBN 1-919798-47-1

29    *The New Brain Drain from Zimbabwe* (2003) ISBN 1-919798-48-X

30    *Regionalizing Xenophobia? Citizen Attitudes to Immigration and Refugee Policy in Southern Africa* (2004) ISBN 1-919798-53-6

31    *Migration, Sexuality and HIV/AIDS in Rural South Africa* (2004) ISBN 1-919798-63-3

32    *Swaziland Moves: Perceptions and Patterns of Modern Migration* (2004) ISBN 1-919798-67-6

33    *HIV/AIDS and Children's Migration in Southern Africa* (2004) ISBN 1-919798-70-6

34    *Medical Leave: The Exodus of Health Professionals from Zimbabwe* (2005) ISBN 1-919798-74-9

35    *Degrees of Uncertainty: Students and the Brain Drain in Southern Africa* (2005) ISBN 1-919798-84-6

36    *Restless Minds: South African Students and the Brain Drain* (2005) ISBN 1-919798-82-X

37    *Understanding Press Coverage of Cross-Border Migration in Southern Africa since 2000* (2005) ISBN 1-919798-91-9

38    *Northern Gateway: Cross-Border Migration Between Namibia and Angola* (2005) ISBN 1-919798-92-7

39    *Early Departures: The Emigration Potential of Zimbabwean Students* (2005) ISBN 1-919798-99-4

40    *Migration and Domestic Workers: Worlds of Work, Health and Mobility in Johannesburg* (2005) ISBN 1-920118-02-0

41    *The Quality of Migration Services Delivery in South Africa* (2005) ISBN 1-920118-03-9

42    *States of Vulnerability: The Future Brain Drain of Talent to South Africa* (2006) ISBN 1-920118-07-1

43    *Migration and Development in Mozambique: Poverty, Inequality and Survival* (2006) ISBN 1-920118-10-1

44    *Migration, Remittances and Development in Southern Africa* (2006) ISBN 1-920118-15-2

45    *Medical Recruiting: The Case of South African Health Care Professionals* (2007) ISBN 1-920118-47-0

46    *Voices From the Margins: Migrant Women's Experiences in Southern Africa* (2007) ISBN 1-920118-50-0

47    *The Haemorrhage of Health Professionals From South Africa: Medical Opinions* (2007) ISBN 978-1-920118-63-1

48    *The Quality of Immigration and Citizenship Services in Namibia* (2008) ISBN 978-1-920118-67-9

49    *Gender, Migration and Remittances in Southern Africa* (2008) ISBN 978-1-920118-70-9

50    *The Perfect Storm: The Realities of Xenophobia in Contemporary South Africa* (2008) ISBN 978-1-920118-71-6

51  *Migrant Remittances and Household Survival in Zimbabwe* (2009) ISBN 978-1-920118-92-1

52  *Migration, Remittances and 'Development' in Lesotho* (2010) ISBN 978-1-920409-26-5

53  *Migration-Induced HIV and AIDS in Rural Mozambique and Swaziland* (2011) ISBN 978-1-920409-49-4

54  *Medical Xenophobia: Zimbabwean Access to Health Services in South Africa* (2011) ISBN 978-1-920409-63-0

55  *The Engagement of the Zimbabwean Medical Diaspora* (2011) ISBN 978-1-920409-64-7

56  *Right to the Classroom: Educational Barriers for Zimbabweans in South Africa* (2011) ISBN 978-1-920409-68-5

57  *Patients Without Borders: Medical Tourism and Medical Migration in Southern Africa* (2012) ISBN 978-1-920409-74-6

58  *The Disengagement of the South African Medical Diaspora* (2012) ISBN 978-1-920596-00-2

59  *The Third Wave: Mixed Migration from Zimbabwe to South Africa* (2012) ISBN 978-1-920596-01-9

60  *Linking Migration, Food Security and Development* (2012) ISBN 978-1-920596-02-6

61  *Unfriendly Neighbours: Contemporary Migration from Zimbabwe to Botswana* (2012) ISBN 978-1-920596-16-3

62  *Heading North: The Zimbabwean Diaspora in Canada* (2012) ISBN 978-1-920596-03-3

63  *Dystopia and Disengagement: Diaspora Attitudes Towards South Africa* (2012) ISBN 978-1-920596-04-0

64  *Soft Targets: Xenophobia, Public Violence and Changing Attitudes to Migrants in South Africa after May 2008* (2013) ISBN 978-1-920596-05-7

65  *Brain Drain and Regain: Migration Behaviour of South African Medical Professionals* (2014) ISBN 978-1-920596-07-1

66  *Xenophobic Violence in South Africa: Denialism, Minimalism, Realism* (2014) ISBN 978-1-920596-08-8

67  *Migrant Entrepreneurship Collective Violence and Xenophobia in South Africa* (2014) ISBN 978-1-920596-09-5

68  *Informal Migrant Entrepreneurship and Inclusive Growth in South Africa, Zimbabwe and Mozambique* (2015) ISBN 978-1-920596-10-1

69  *Calibrating Informal Cross-Border Trade in Southern Africa* (2015) ISBN 978-1-920596-13-2

Printed in the United States
By Bookmasters